George Tremlett has been a rock writer almost since the music began in the mid-fifties. He left King Edward VI School, Stratford-upon-Avon, in 1957 and then spent four years on the *Coventry Evening Telegraph* writing their daily TV column and reviewing all the visiting pop package shows. In 1961 he moved to London and became a freelance writer, working part-time for *The New Musical Express*. He has since been London correspondent for TV and pop music magazines in Japan, Holland, Sweden, the United States, Belgium, Germany, Australia, New Zealand and Finland. In this he is partnered by his wife, Jane. They have also contributed to most major British teenage magazines. Outside pop music journalism, George Tremlett pursues a political career as a member of the Greater London Council. For eleven years he was also a councillor in Richmond-upon-Thames.

D1437999

Also by George Tremlett

George Tremlett

The Queen Story

Futura Publications Limited
A Futura Book

A Futura Book

First published in Great Britain in 1976
by Futura Publications Limited

Copyright © George Tremlett Ltd 1976

ISBN 0 8600 7412 9

Printed in Great Britain by
Hazell Watson & Viney Ltd
Aylesbury, Bucks

Futura Publications Limited
110 Warner Road
Camberwell, London SE5

ACKNOWLEDGEMENTS

My thanks are due to a number of people who have explained so much that was unknown until now about Queen: to Norman Sheffield, whose companies financed the group's first success; to Dave Thomas, their co-manager for two years; to publicist Tony Brainsby; to Alan Mair; to Brian May's parents, Harold and Ruth May; to John Bagnall, label manager for EMI Records; to Pat and Sue Johnstone, who run the Queen Fan Club; to David Croker, now managing director at Rocket Records, and to Tim Staffell, the original singer with the group Smile that begat Queen.

CHAPTER ONE

Queen's success story is something quite new in British rock music. In a very short time they have become one of the world's leading groups – from only four LPs and five singles (each of which was taken from the album material), and a sense of theatre that gives them a stunning stage presence. It has all happened over a period of little more than two years.

Recording their four albums and spending seven months of each year travelling from concert hall to concert hall – that's all Queen's story really amounts to in conventional rock legend terms. They have never had to sweat it out in the cellars of Hamburg or Merseyside; they have never had to starve for their art; there have been no personal tragedies to overcome; they have not experienced the transition from teenybop act to world rock stardom – and so there are hardly any skeletons in their cupboard. And because they do not have this background in sixties pop music that the Stones and The Beatles, The Faces and Led Zeppelin, Deep Purple and 10cc, Gary Glitter and David Bowie all had, very little is known about Queen. It has been their good fortune to reach the top at a time when the good musicians no longer have to tell the world all about their private lives. All that is secret now; the music is all that matters – or, at least, that's what the music papers try to tell us.

In fact, Queen's image has been carefully cultivated. The story is – and it is a true story – that the group grew out of the *mélange* of musicians, actors, art students and clothes-makers who all ran tiny stalls at the Kensington Market in the late sixties and early seventies, selling suede boots, old clothes, velvet dresses and jackets – anything that would turn a fast quid in the name of fashion.

Against that background, it seemed totally natural that Freddie Mercury should be a Queen of high camp with his swirling silk stage clothes and black-painted fingernails, his silver rings and bracelets and extravagant gestures to his 'Dears' and 'Darlings' in the audience. As the name 'Queen' and the image that they project were originally wholly his ideas and because he is up-front selling it all like a tart, the whole creation ripples and washes over the rest of the group.

And yet actually their story runs much deeper than that.

It is a fascinating story, and in this book which is based on exclusive interviews with people who have known them at every stage in their career, from those who worked in the market to the record business executives in the higher echelons of rock finance, you will see how it is possible in the seventies for four talented people to reach the top in a very short time, and how the businessmen of rock recognise new talent when it appears and use their skills to ensure that the talent is acclaimed.

In part, it is a story of what money can do for rock music – but it is also a very personal, revealing account of what happens to people when success comes suddenly, and this is why in the chapters that follow I quote directly from the people I have spoken to rather than interpret their interviews with me in the third person.

Our story really begins with two people, although it should be said at the outset that in no sense do I underestimate the skills either of Queen's bass player John Deacon or of Roger Meddows Taylor, who is one of the more gentle and expressive drummers that rock music has produced. Their talents are essential to the success of the group as a whole, but in Freddie Mercury and Brian May we have two of the finest and most unusual songwriters to have come to the fore in recent years. Their styles are very different.

Mercury is provocative and challenging with strange changes of melody and a potency in his lyric-writing that makes one think of Lennon or Bowie. Indeed, it is Mercury's writing that has so far brought Queen most of their success, he wrote their three major hit singles 'Seven Seas Of Rhye', 'Killer Queen' and 'Bohemian Rhapsody', the song that was number one in all the British music paper charts for eight weeks towards the end of 1975 and early 1976, and it is he who composed two of their

8

major stage numbers, 'Liar' and 'In The Lap Of The Gods'. There is also a gentle side to Mercury's writing that one heard on songs like 'Seaside Rendezvous' (a personal favourite of mine) and 'Lazing On A Sunday Afternoon' on the recent album *A Night At The Opera.*

For a group to possess a writer of Mercury's distinction is rare enough, but in Brian May Queen have another composer with a very different, almost McCartney-style talent. In fact, there was one song ('Good Company'), on the LP *A Night At The Opera* on which May played nearly all the instruments, creating a jazz band effect, which sounded almost pure McCartney to me. And there's nothing derogatory in saying that because the song was new and complete, it was the style that was McCartney. And in his other writing May has shown that his range of writing is very considerable – it was he who wrote 'Now I'm Here', the number with which Queen have so often opened their stage act, 'The Prophet's Song', which is as chilling as any of Bowie's most urgent work, the group's first single 'Keep Yourself Alive', the striking 'Procession' or the stunning 'Brighton Rock' on which his range as a guitarist is so wide and inventive that one begins to compare his talents with those of Clapton, Page or Hendrix.

Just as Lennon and McCartney achieved so much more in the earliest stages of their careers working together within The Beatles than they could ever have done by starting off solo, so Mercury and May have fused together within Queen, not pretending to write together but underlaying each other's talents so that you hear Mercury creating an electric effect when their stage act opens in total darkness with him singing the May song 'Now I'm Here' or May's guitar work so complimenting a song like Mercury's 'Killer Queen' with soaring notes of great purity. It is a true marriage of talents such as one rarely finds in music.

The strange thing is that Mercury and May grew up in the Western suburbs of London with their homes little more than a hundred yards apart without them ever meeting until Mercury had taken a stall in Kensington Market. Indeed, their

9

parents did not meet for the first time until both Mr and Mrs Bulsara (Freddie's real name) and Mr and Mrs May both went along to a Queen concert at Hammersmith Odeon during their autumn tour in 1975.

When I first heard of this odd coincidence, I decided to investigate it as fully as I could, thinking at first that there could be some strange background to Queen's success that had never been reported; that perhaps they had not come together through the Kensington Market at all, but had like so many other groups been friends in childhood – and that the whole Kensington Market saga was nothing more than a good bit of image-building.

But, no – my suspicions were all ill-founded, although it must be said that I do have the impression that Freddie Mercury has gone to considerable lengths to conceal his own background. When he has been asked his own name, he has been evasive; one journalist was told it was 'Pluto'! Even Tony Brainsby, who was Queen's personal publicist for three years until they left Trident's management and switched to John Reid, told me that he had no idea what Mercury's real name was. 'One of the first times he came to my office, he told me what his name was – but that was the only time it was ever mentioned,' said Brainsby, who thought it sounded Polish.

In fact, as I say, Mercury's real name is Bulsara. His father works as an accounts clerk and his name is Bomi Bulsara and he lives with his wife, Jer B. Bulsara, in the Feltham district of Hounslow, which was where I confirmed their names in the local electoral records. The family home is a tiny, semi-detached Victorian house almost beneath the take-off route from Heathrow Airport; an immaculately-kept artisan cottage with a recently-added front porch extension and a separate side entrance down a passageway. After the family had arrived in England, it was there that Freddie spent his teens, living at home with his sister Kashmira, who is some six years younger than he is and who is now married to a sales representative, Roger Cooke, and living in the North of England.

Hoping that the Bulsaras would be willing to talk to me

about Freddie's childhood and his early days as a musician, I called round at the house and they both came to the door.

'Are you Mrs Bulsara?' I asked, and she confirmed that she was.

'And are you Mr Bulsara?' I added, and he agreed.

So then I explained that I was writing a book on Queen, and before I could say any more Mrs Bulsara said, smiling: 'That has nothing to do with us. Why do you want to speak to us?'

'But Freddie Mercury – he is your son, Freddie Bulsara,' I said, and at first she appeared to be saying that it all had nothing to do with them at all, and then when I repeated the name 'Freddie Bulsara' they both smiled very politely and said: 'Yes, that is true. We have got all his photographs and stories – but we don't want to talk about it. We do not want to get involved in all that.'

It has always been my view that if people do not want to be interviewed, they have a perfect right to refuse – but I still had the feeling at the back of my mind that living so close to the May family, there could be this possibility that Freddie Bulsara and Brian May had been friends in childhood and that all the stories told about Kensington Market were just an elaborately constructed camouflage (that may sound suspicious, but I have been writing about rock music long enough to be fairly cautious about most stories I am told!).

So then I walked little more than a hundred yards, crossing the main road to the airport, to the house where Brian May lived throughout his childhood, and which is still his parents' home. There I had a long detailed conversation with Mr and Mrs May, which filled in many of the gaps that appear in all other published accounts of Queen's early days – and made it quite clear that it really was nothing more than a very strange coincidence that Mercury and May should have grown up so close together without becoming friends until years later.

Although Mercury is the extrovert showman who gives Queen so much of their charisma as a live group, it has always been the musicianship of Brian May that has been Queen's pivotal strength; it has been his home-made guitar that has produced so many of the sound effects that make their records so distinctive, and as I have mentioned as a musician he is already being compared with Clapton, Page and Hendrix as one of the true guitar superstars. Quite clearly, although he is shy and retiring, May is becoming one of the more important figures in rock music – and after talking to his parents I was left in no doubt that it is his family background, and the way that he has always shared an interest in electronics with his father, that has given him and hence Queen their difference in musical outlook.

Brian Harold May was born in a nursing home at Hampton Hill, Twickenham, on July 19th, 1947, to Ruth May and her husband Harold. The family home was then and is still a semi-detached, typically thirties-style house in Feltham, just over the border from Twickenham. Mr May is an electronics engineer working for the Ministry of Defence; a man whose work suits his personality, being precise in all he says and does.

I spoke to him and his wife in their living room while Squeaky, Brian's black-and-ginger cat, crawled around my shoulders; they were looking after Squeaky while Brian toured the United States with Queen.

They recalled how Brian had gone to Hanworth Road state primary school, winning a scholarship at the age of eleven to Hampton Grammar School, an old-established school recognised as one of the best academically in London. 'Hampton was three miles away, and he used to travel there every day on his bike, which is still out there in the garage, rusting away,' said Mr May.

At Hampton, Brian May proved to be an outstanding scholar, with passes in ten subjects at the Ordinary level of the General Certificate of Education and then later three passes at Advanced level. Very much with his father's approval, he went on to study at Imperial College, Kensington, gaining an honours degree in physics and maths and training himself for a career as an infra red astronomer. Subsequently he was personally invited by Professor Sir Bernard Lovell to work at the Jodrell Bank Laboratory while preparing his thesis to become a doctor of philosophy, but rather than break up the group he was then playing in, May stayed at Imperial College and continued studying for his doctorate there.

'He was preparing a thesis on zodiacal light, which are great showers of particles that can be seen at sunset and sunrise and which have never been satisfactorily explained,' said Mr May. 'Before Queen started to become successful, he was doing private tutorials at Imperial College, and had also had constructed to his own designs special apparatus for the study of zodiacal light which had been shipped out to Tenerife in the Canary Islands so that observations could be recorded . . . he has never given up his studies, and whenever I see him he keeps telling me that he needs only three months' work to complete his thesis, which he temporarily put aside around the time of the *Queen II* album. He has actually written the thesis, but it needs to be revised and finalised and then typed up with certain data included.'

It was that second album, *Queen II*, that finally convinced Mr May that his son really had something to contribute to music; until then, he admits there had been a little tension in the family because Mr and Mrs May – quite understandably – thought it tragic that such a promising scientific career might be jeopardised for something as nebulous as a musician's life.

'All through his childhood, music had been Brian's main hobby, but we had thought of it only as a hobby even though we are a musical family,' said Mr May, who himself collects rock music albums along with works by Mahler and other classical composers.

'About the time of *Queen II* we started to see the possibilities that the group had, musically,' said Mr May. 'We still think that *Queen II* was a masterpiece – and that's why Brian gave us the gold disc he got from that album to hang on the wall. We felt that that album contained much of the group's most emotional and heart-felt music, and to us it is full of obvious tracks of teenage conflict like "Father To Son", which Brian wrote . . . I think all teenagers have emotional conflicts, and we can hear it in that song.'

Brian had formed his first group while still at Hampton Grammar School. It was called 1984, and although he has long since left it the group is still performing on an amateur basis around pubs and other venues in West London. The other members of that group were Tim Staffell, who later went on to become the singer with Brian's second group, Smile; John Garnham, who usually played bass; Dave Dilloway, who played rhythm guitar and Richard Thompson, their drummer.

'Brian had been interested in music ever since he was a child,' said Mr May. 'When he was seven we bought him his first small acoustic guitar, and then later he started taking piano lessons at a school in Baker Street going right through to the fourth or fifth grade, although he never became a professional musician until Queen.

'That group 1984 was just a school group, and then while he was with Smile he was a student so they were never more than semi-professional . . . when he was in 1984, I used to drive them to their gigs sometimes in my old Javelin, with microphone stands sticking out of the back windows because they were too long to fit in the back of the car. I suppose I must have stood in the wings and watched them play about a dozen times.

'During the week he would have to spend nearly all his evenings at home studying for his exams, and he was always very conscientious about that, but at the weekends he'd be off to play at different places with the group. That was his main outlet; music and swimming were the only outside relaxations that he ever had . . . 1984 used to play mainly at small local dance halls, pubs and boating clubs.

'The boating clubs at Putney and Sunbury were two of the places where they used to appear regularly, and they're gigs that he still remembers with pleasure because they'd carry on playing until two in the morning, by which time everyone would be very merry and swinging from the chandeliers. They used to dress in old Army jackets with brass buttons, which were all the vogue at the time though most illegal, and their music consisted of the hits of the day interspersed with some of their own writing.

14

'The one number that Brian used to play which was always a great show-stopper, though it is something that he has still never recorded, was something that he used to call the "Happy Hendrix Polka". He was always influenced by Jimi Hendrix, who was the God in those days although we ourselves weren't very much into music at that time, and this was a number that the group would introduce with a claim that it had been recorded at some specially speeded-up level, although in fact it was just Brian playing guitar at record speed . . . and then there was another jokey sort of number where a big spider would descend on the stage while they sang another thing they'd written called "Itsy Bitsy Spider", which was always one of the great favourites at all the boat club parties . . .'

Even though Brian May had been given a small acoustic guitar when he was seven, he had never moved on to the conventional Fender electric instruments; right from the start of the group 1984 he always played a guitar that he had made at home with his father which incorporated many electrical ideas of their own.

Having always been keen on anything electronic, Mr May had converted the small bedroom at his home into a workshop and it was there that father and son worked together, constructing the instrument that Brian May has used throughout his career as a musician, both in the recording studio and in all their stage appearances.

'Initially, they started it as something to do together because they were both keen on making things,' said Brian's mother.

'Even as a little child, Brian had always had this analytical approach to the things. You remember those little wooden puzzles in which dozens of little pieces that all look very similar slot together to form a model? Well, we once had a whole pack of those and Brian would dismantle them all, pile all the bits and pieces together, and then time himself and re-assemble the whole lot in about half an hour . . . he had the sort of mind that liked to deal with a challenge like that. Later still, after he had become interested in astronomy and was watching all those

Patrick Moore programmes on TV, he and his father constructed their own four-inch telescope.

'We'd bought him that small acoustic guitar when he was younger, but we really couldn't afford to buy him a proper electric one when The Beatles became all the rage, and so he and his father made their own guitar, working in the evenings in the workshop through Brian's third and fourth years at school. It took them two years to complete it – at a total cost of some eight pounds.'

Mrs May produced a series of photographs that Brian had taken himself at the time he was working on the instrument, during 1963 and 1964, showing how he had assembled the guitar, stage by stage, and they prove, if any proof be needed, that it really is a most remarkable instrument.

The body of the guitar, coloured a deep red, he carved himself from a solid piece of wood which for the previous hundred years had been part of a fireplace. He shaped the neck with a penknife. Noticing that with so many modern electric guitars the tension placed on the strings was so great that it tended to bend the instruments' necks, Brian and his father designed a neck that incorporated a steel truss rod – and it is still rigidly in place to this day, thirteen years after they designed it.

'We calculated that tightening the strings introduced a stress that was equal to three and a half hundredweight, and under that sort of strain it's not surprising that the necks bend,' said Mr May. 'So we introduced our own truss rod, setting it at an opposite angle to the tension through the neck of the guitar, holding it in place with a steel bolt . . . then Brian persuaded his mother to give him the mother of pearl buttons in her button box, and with those he made his own fret-board . . . then we designed our own adjustable bridge, which was designed to overcome another problem.

'We realised that with many guitars when the strings were tightened over the bridge when you used the tremolo arm, this had the effect of sawing away at the strings making it possible that the string would snap; so instead of a conventional bridge we designed a set of small rollers, which can have the

strings tightened over them without the same wear and tear . . .
this was a good idea because it means that the strings keep their
tone longer, and also last longer.

'Another problem that we tried to solve was that with many
guitars when you adjust the tremolo, it doesn't always go back to
the place where it was before – and that can be responsible for
making the guitar go out of tune . . . so we fitted two motorbike
valve springs which I found in a 1928 Panther bike, and these
balance the tremolo arm perfectly. Then instead of having a
set of factory made pick-ups, Brian built his own, using a little
Meccano wheel which we built to wind around 4,000 turns of
wire on each of the three pick-ups. The secret of these pick-ups
is in the position that each one is set because this alters the tonal
harmonic effect, and by some really clever switching you can
have any combination of twenty-four tones – and that's something that no other guitar manufacturer has ever done commercially at all. When he plays that solo on "Brighton Rock",
Brian is accompanying himself, using echoes . . .'

Father and son also designed special 'acoustic pockets',
which are designed to help the air resonate around the middle
of the guitar's frequency range – which accentuates the feedback
effects that Brian can achieve with the instrument. And then
having constructed a guitar that had a tonal range and depth
far beyond that of most commercially marketed instruments,
Brian and his father went on to build amplifiers and a tape
echo unit.

Brian explained the significance of some of this in an interview with the magazine *Guitar*: 'You know, you can play electric guitar in three ways: first as an amplified acoustic guitar,
at fairly low volume, with all the natural decay of notes. Then
you can turn it up to the level where the feedback just about
counteracts the friction in the system so you can sustain the note
indefinitely – the sort of Clapton thing. Or you can go one stage
further and turn it up so that the loop is greater than One:
then the thing is bursting forth of its own accord all the time.
That's the sort of level I like to play at. But it's got to burst
forth at the frequencies you want it to burst forth, not with

17

some nasty whistle somewhere up the top. It all depends on not having microphonic pick-ups: it's got to feed back through the strings, not direct through the pick-ups. So these things are all damped by embedding them (the pick-ups) in Araldite . . .'

All this is highly technical, as indeed were the descriptions of what they had done together given me by Brian May's father – but this mastery that he has of every aspect of his instrument and the equipment available in the recording studio is what has enabled Queen to achieve such a pure and different sound. It is no exaggeration to say that Queen, and May in particular, have introduced totally new techniques into rock music; whereas the first British rock musicians were untrained musicians who had learnt their instruments the hard way in the grimy netherland of provincial clubs and ballrooms, Queen are bringing to the music skills that are essentially those of the trained engineer. And yet it is still music, and very fine music, with its range of melody and lyrical content.

'In that first group, 1984, I think Brian was just conquering his instrument and learning all the things that go to make up a band – I think people often overlook the thought that goes into music,' said Mr May, who although a scientist by training has the fine, expressive hands of an artist.

'I think there's a lot of The Beatles' influence in Queen's music, but there's also a classical influence . . . I have listened to some of their material and heard Mahler's Choral Symphony deep down in there somewhere. That's one of the beauties and joys of music. The tapestry is laid down for you and then once you have mastered your own instrument you put your own thoughts into the music . . . that's what so annoys me about the critics in the music papers. I don't know how they manage to write the things that they do. They seem to me to be total morons, although I must say that the critics never worry Brian. Nothing worries Brian. Right from the very beginning of it all, money hasn't interested him at all – he has a total involvement in the music itself. That's always been the only thing that has mattered to him, the music.

'And, of course, this is something that he grew up with as a child,' said Mr May, who as well as being so interested in the mechanics of sound also played piano and ukulele himself.

'I was never a professional musician; the only times I've ever played in public were in the school band and in the Air Force during the war when I used to take my ukulele down to the pub – that's the same old ukulele, a genuine "George Formby uke", that Brian still plays now when he uses a ukulele on stage with Queen. It's full of beer stains inside from the war days, but Brian still insists that it's got the best sound he's ever heard from a ukulele, although he also uses a little Japanese one which he was presented with there when they were touring Japan. It was on that ukulele that he learned to play and sing his first songs, old George Formby music hall numbers like "Cleaning Windows", "Leaning On The Lamp-post" and "Chinese Laundry Blues" – I taught them all to him. Then he started developing techniques of his own which were remarkably like George Formby's . . . he also used to play the mouth organ and when he joined the school choir, he used to practise like mad for that.

'He's always had this interest in anything to do with music; he's taught himself to play tin whistles, the Jew's harp, and when he felt they needed a harp-effect on *A Night At The Opera*, he went out and bought himself a harp and taught himself to play. He's always had this thing about mastering every instrument . . . for me the most remarkable thing he's done so far with Queen was that track on *A Night At The Opera* which he wrote himself, "Good Company". Everything we did in making that guitar together can be heard on that track on which he plays ukulele and guitar, and by using a twenty-four-track recorder manages to make his guitar sound like trombones, cellos and piccolos – the whole thing is just him. Anyone who can't appreciate an achievement of that kind must be a musical moron . . . and to him it is all so satisfying, scientifically.'

Although they had always shared these interests in electronics and in music, Mr May had never thought through Brian's childhood that his son would become a musician, and this also came as a surprise to Mrs May. 'We had always thought that music would become a life-long hobby; it never crossed our minds that he might make it his career,' she said.

Instead, his parents believed that Brian May would go on to gain his doctorate in philosophy, quite possibly becoming one of the country's leading infra-red astronomers.

'In the holidays, when he was broke and waiting for his next term's grant to arrive, Brian used to come back here and take temporary jobs just so that he'd have some money of his own coming in . . . he spent a fortnight making windscreen wipers and then in one summer recess spent two months working at EMI Electronics assessing the destructive effect of fragmentation bombs, which he found interesting from a mathematical point of view – although he was really horrified by the work itself. He was none too happy to be working away at maximising the killing effects of bombs . . . and then another time he took a job in an accountant's office, and after Queen had actually signed with Trident and were waiting for everything to happen he took a teaching job at a comprehensive school near Brixton Oval, where most of the kids were coloured. He taught there for three or four months just after the first Queen album had been released, and got the most glowing references when he left. The headmaster didn't want him to leave because Brian seemed to really identify with the children that he was teaching and their problems.'

It is quite clear from the way that Mr and Mrs May talked that at that stage Queen were by no means sure that the group would become as successful as they hoped it would. They were ambitious – but none too optimistic. Brian had his occasional jobs to bring in extra money and would quite probably have continued teaching at that school if the *Queen II* album had not been so successful. Roger and Freddie still kept on their stall in Kensington Market for some time after Freddie had left his other group and joined Brian and Roger to form Queen, and Freddie stayed on in the market even after Roger had left and taken a flat in Richmond while studying botany at Kew Gardens, and even after John Deacon completed what was to be their final line-up he continued to teach in a comprehensive school.

When he returned to his parents' home in Feltham, Brian May would tell them: 'I am either going to get to the top – or chuck it!'

'They all had that sort of determination to get to the top and a total belief in what they were doing musically, but I think they were quite realistic about the odds that were stacked against them,' said Mr May.

'We were a little worried at that stage that he was spending so much time on music, although I think I was more worried about the effect of losing sleep and the crude travelling arrangements they had when they did go on those trips down to Cornwall – I think all parents worry about their children's safety, and it was nothing more than that. When he was staying in Barnes, we used to sometimes drive round there with a change of clothes and things like that, and I remember us arriving there one afternoon and Brian introducing us to Roger and Freddie Mercury, and sitting there while they talked about all the plans they had for Queen. They were all wearing velvet jackets and flared trousers when they appeared on stage then, and they were discussing ideas for the sort of stage clothes that they have now . . . in all the pads that Brian used to stay in, there were all their guitars and drum kits lying around the place, and we used to hear bits and pieces as they talked, and put it all together when we got home as parents do.

'That was during the summer of 1971 when Brian, Freddie and Roger were talking about their plans, and John Deacon hadn't come along then – in fact, we still haven't met John Deacon although we've had all the other members of the group sitting in our front room at different times. Even then, the three of them seemed very closely knit. They are very dissimilar people, with Freddie so much more extrovert and having that extravagant way of expressing himself whereas Brian has always been the very opposite . . . but even in those days, when we used to talk to them over in Barnes they were always talking as though everything they had to do would have to be perfect, and that nothing else would do. I think that's the bond that they have in common – the pursuit of excellence.'

Since then, Mr and Mrs May have attended all Queen's London concerts – and being Brian's parents has brought them into a strange sort of limelight that they never expected to live in. 'We get people phoning us all the time and asking if Brian is in,' said Mr May. 'And when we went to that first concert at the Hammersmith Odeon when they were supporting Mott the Hoople, a very strange thing happened. We had seats down at the front and we'd never been to a concert like that before, and I suppose at our age we must have looked a little out of place. Anyway, there was a young man sitting in front of me who suddenly turned round and said: "Who's Dad are you, then?" He was an out-and-out Mott the Hoople fan, but when I explained that Brian May was my son he handed me his programme and asked me to sign it. "Don't be silly – I'm just a humble civil servant," I said, but he insisted –and then asked me to put "Brian May's Dad" in brackets after I'd autographed his programme.'

Brian's mother had an even stranger experience when a woman she knew came into the shop where she works in Hounslow, holding the hand of her very young daughter who said: 'You're Brian's Mum, aren't you – do you mind if I touch you?'

In the main, though – apart from comments from friends at work who keep talking to him about Queen's success – very little of their day-to-day excitement overlaps into the May's home. 'We still see a lot of Brian, just as we did when he was at college,' said Mr May. 'He brought his cat round here before going off on their latest US tour, and he also asked me to look after his car. He's got the most fabulous car – a Volvo 1800, the sort of car that Roger Moore used to drive in "The Saint" series on television. It's an absorbing car to play with; it's got fuel injection, which means that the petrol is fed electronically – I've had all that to pieces several times while he's been away to see how it works, and there are a few faults in the engine which I've been trying to cure for him while he's away.'

Looking ahead, I asked Mr May how he thought his son's career might develop. 'I think that largely depends on how the group's fans react to their music,' he said. 'For the past two years, he's had hardly any spare time at all, but as soon as he has some spare time I should think he'll finish his thesis for his doctorate because he is the sort of person who never likes to leave anything unfinished. And then after that it depends how much money there is. If the money is there, I am sure he would like to build his own private research laboratory . . . we've talked of patenting some of the ideas that we've worked on together for guitars and other instruments, and music is something that never comes to an end. There is always something new to do.'

CHAPTER TWO

One of Brian May's closest friends at Hampton Grammar
School was Tim Staffell, who was the singer with the group
1984 for some four years. That band broke up when May went
on to Imperial College to pursue his other ambition of becoming an infra-red astronomer and Staffell moved to Ealing
College of Art to study graphics. But being friends, they kept
in close touch and when May formed Smile in came Staffell as
singer, often bringing an art college friend along to their gigs –
Freddie Mercury.

'I suppose Smile must have lasted for another three years
and it wasn't until I left in 1970 that Freddie, Roger and
Brian came together and formed Queen,' said Staffell, who
now lives in St Margarets, East Twickenham, which was where
he and I had a long discussion covering the history of the two
groups and his friendship with May, Mercury and Taylor during this crucial period.

'The thing that started Brian and I off at Hampton was that
there was already another group at the school called The
Others, who had appeared on TV and who were at that time
every bit as good as the Rolling Stones, who were also playing
in the clubs around that area,' said Staffell. 'They were quite
successful, and a music thing started going at the school; they
were certainly the kind of figures who made a deep impression
on their contemporaries, and made us all want to be as good as
them.'

This was further accentuated by the fact that Paul Samwell-
Smith, bass guitarist and musical director with The Yardbirds
and more recently record producer for Cat Stevens, had also
been to Hampton – and so had another member of The Yardbirds, Jim McCarty.

'With The Yardbirds doing so well and making records, and
The Others also apparently on the brink of things although they

eventually gave it all up to concentrate on their studies, there was a very strong feeling for music running through the school,' said Staffell. 'It meant that there was something else going on there over and above the normal life of the school, which was a total drag as far as I was concerned, anyway ... it was a very repressive sort of institution, and for me being in a group was a way to escape from all that.

'The Others were very much like the Rolling Stones. They really were a very good band, and most people thought they were more polished than the Stones, who were playing every week at that time at the Station Hotel in Richmond ... there was a lot of music going on all round the area, and Brian and I and all our friends used to go to all these different pubs, clubs and youth clubs to see who was doing what. We used to see a lot of The Yardbirds and then there were The Muleskinners, who then had Eric Clapton as their lead guitarist – I saw them playing at the Richmond Community Centre ... and then there were The Bullets, who were also very good, The Five Proud Walkers, Chris and The Whirlwinds, Jo Jo Gunne and The Birds, which Ron Wood of The Faces used to be in in those days ... The Who had also started playing in the same clubs, and Townshend had just left the Ealing art college when I went there, although I didn't see The Who live until they were at The Marquee.

'To us being at a very traditional grammar school like Hampton, all this was marvellous. There were so many places to go to every weekend ... there was The Beachcomber Club at London Airport, where I often used to see John Mayall and another very good little band called The Chains. It was such a contrast to the drudgery of school, which I always found pretty intolerable.'

When 1984 was formed, Staffell became the singer; Brian May, lead guitarist; John Garnham, bass guitarist; Dave Dilloway, rhythm guitarist, and Richard Thompson – the only member who did not go to the Hampton school – became their drummer.

'We started our rehearsals at a school in Whitton next to the

Twickenham rugby ground,' said Staffell. 'Every time I go into a school building now it is very evocative, because we spent so many of our evenings going into that place and learning to play our instruments . . . we didn't have to pay anything to play there. So many groups were getting formed at that time that it was decided to let them use this school to rehearse because it was somewhere that one could play without disturbing any neighbours.

'The first gig we played was at St Mary's church hall near the centre of Twickenham, not very far from Eel Pie Island. I'll always remember that night because we had a guy playing with us who had built his own organ, and you've never seen such a thing in your life – he had taken a harmonica attached to a small electric blower, which may have been a hair drier unit, and then added his own small keyboard.

'We used to do a very wide range of material, using Everly Brothers' songs with much more involved harmonies than other bands were using – songs like "Dream", which we faithfully tried to reproduce. Then we did The Beatles, "Help" with three-part harmonies, with Brian coming in, and other songs of theirs like "I Should Have Known Better", "I'm A Loser" and "She's A Woman". We used to play considerably longer than most bands did – often as long as three hours at gigs like the Thames Boat Club in Putney, which was one of our regular gigs.

'When Jimi Hendrix came along we started playing his material because it had become pretty evident that Brian was a much finer guitarist than you'd find in most little groups and numbers like "Stone Free", "Purple Haze" and "Hey Joe" gave him an opportunity to show what he could do . . . but we always tried to add little bits of our own. There was one number we did, "She's Gone" which was recorded by Buddy Knox, to which we added our own arrangement, too, adding a little bit at the end from that song about "The grandfather clock which stopped short, never to go again . . ." And then we'd stop suddenly ourselves on the word "again", which always drew a round of applause because audiences weren't used to local groups being able to stop suddenly like that for effect. Brian May used to work on ideas like that, and we were very proud of them.

'In those days, the group tended to play just at the week-ends because we all had our school work to do during the week. But it was varied. Occasionally, we would play three times a week – and then other times we'd just have three bookings in a month. But it was always something that we were committed to; even when we didn't have a booking, it was still our group and we'd rehearse.

'Once we went in for a talent contest at the Top Rank in Croydon, playing in two capacities that night. In one spot the group played without me backing a singer called Liza Perez, and then we did our own spot – and won. We were each presented with a reel of tape and a CBS album – I picked Simon and Garfunkel's – although the reels of tape were useless because none of us owned tape recorders in those days.

'I can remember that day extremely well because that was when I commenced my first serious romantic involvement which lasted for four years and then broke up with heartbreak all round. We did four numbers, "So Sad", although I can't remember who wrote that; "Stone Free", which was a Hendrix composition; "She's Gone" by Buddy Knox and "Knock On Wood" by Eddie Floyd. I was wearing a blue shirt with pink polka dots, the drummer was wearing a shirt of silver silk, and Brian had one of those blue serge Royal Marines' jackets that he'd picked up at the Antique Market in Chelsea. Old uniforms were all the rage in those days, and he'd dressed himself up so that he looked like a 1920's policeman ... it was a great excitement when we won, but nothing happened after that. It didn't lead to a recording contract or anything like that.

'Carrying our equipment around used to be quite a problem because we didn't have a van then, but John Garnham had one of those tiny Heinkel bubble cars and I can remember travelling around in that with the roof off with all our gear and microphone stands sticking out of the top ... we used to go round to each other's homes and practise before some of our bookings just so that we could try out any new ideas that we'd had, and I think that the most we ever got paid was about thirty pounds. That would have been the absolute ceiling – usually we only got about fifteen pounds a night, but that would be immediately split between the five of us which meant that we were quite well off for schoolboys, although money was never the main attraction.

'One particularly good gig we played was at Wargrave on Henley Regatta Day. When we got there, they'd laid out some beautiful food for us, a terrific salad and free beer. We played our set and we'd had a few drinks and when it came to the last number I remember saying: "Don't clap – just throw us some money!" And they showered us with silver and ten bob notes. We must have each picked up another two pounds that night.

'Another of the places that we used to play occasionally was the Feltham R & B Club, which was just behind the old cinema in Feltham. Those nights we used to include more of our rhythm 'n' blues material like Chuck Berry's "Our Little Rendezvous" and "Too Much Monkey Business", and Bo Diddley's "I'm A Man" (which is not to be confused with the thing that Spencer Davis did) although we also did the Spencer Davis number "Keep On Running" and a song that was recorded by The Three Caps, "Cool Jerk", along with the standards like "Land Of A Thousand Dances". We had a very wide repertoire even though we only played at week-ends because there was pretty severe if slightly concealed disapproval from my parents, if not the others' parents, about the whole thing.

'Occasionally, we'd play a few ballads; Brian used to sing "Yesterday" which used to get screams and applause, and made me dead jealous. At places like the Thames Boat Club the audience basically just wanted a beat group and something to dance to and have a good time, but every now and then if you could include a number like that, which people identified with, it would draw a different sort of response ... "Yesterday" always went down very well.'

Brian May was a year ahead of Tim Staffell at Hampton

Grammar School, and so left the school earlier to go on to Imperial College while Staffell stayed on another seven or eight months, eventually leaving mid-term and going on to Ealing College of Art. 'We'd become close friends by that time, and even while Brian was starting at Imperial he used to call round at my house or I'd call round at his and we'd write songs together,' said Staffell. 'Our ideas had become more sophisticated, and with other members of the group also leaving school and going their separate ways 1984 sort of disintegrated. When he got to Imperial, Brian put an advertisement on the college notice board for a drummer and that was how he met Roger Meddows Taylor, who was then still at dental college although he was going round to all the concerts at different colleges in London.'

Roger Meddows Taylor had been born at King's Lynn in Norfolk, and then when he was eight he and his sister Clare had moved down to Truro in Cornwall with their parents and Roger had gone to the Truro Cathedral School, singing in the cathedral choir for a year. Then at the age of eleven he had gone to the local public school, Truro School, although not as a boarder but as a day-boy. He has since said that he hated school and 'really felt sorry for the boarders who hardly ever saw their homes. I would've hated to board myself because it would have given me no freedom at all, and I was always in and out of semi-pro groups.' He took up the guitar and then later drums, and after passing in seven subjects at O-level and then in Biology, Chemistry and Physics at A-level he went up to London to train to become a dentist at the London Dental School (that's the name by which it is popularly known among students; the correct name is the London Hospital Medical College in Whitechapel). There, he found himself examining corpses and doing a whole range of studies that he found bordering on the unpleasant – and so he left and took a stall in Kensington Market which he ran with Freddie Mercury with whom he also shared a flat.

After running the stall for nearly two years, he went off to the North London Polytechnic to take a course in biology, eventually taking his degree. Tim Staffell knew him throughout this period, and indeed was largely responsible for bringing Roger, Freddie and Brian together, but first hear what Roger himself told me about that stall he ran in Kensington Market:

'We used to sell lovely old velvet stuff with lace and also lots of old clothes which Freddie and I used to pick up going round rag merchants and junk yards. The biggest stroke of luck that we ever had was when we bought a hundred fur coats from a rag merchant in Battersea for fifty pence each – and then sold them all for between four and eight pounds. And that was still a bargain that we were offering; you can't buy a second-hand fur coat today for under twenty pounds. Then we had another good buy in forty Russian fox furs. When we bought those, we had our own full length black velvet coats made up, and then trimmed each one with fox fur. And they looked beautiful when we were ready to sell them.

'We kept the stall on for about eighteen months, paying a rent of ten pounds a week and those were good days with us making a good living and enjoying ourselves because the market was run by musicians, actors, writers and artists; the sort of people who had ideas of their own but who needed some little sideline like that to bring in some extra money. Then there'd always be people from different groups wandering around the market looking for clothes, and sometimes we'd serve film stars like Julie Christie. It was almost a life-style of its own with quite a few eccentrics. Now, that's all changed. Instead, it's run by the usual sort of people who run clothes and shoe shops and sell manufactured products.'

Tim Staffell had actually come to know Freddie Mercury even before he set up that stall in the market with Roger Meddows Taylor. When Staffell arrived at the Ealing College of Art he was in the same class taking the graphics course as Freddie Mercury, and by an odd coincidence one of their teachers was my brother-in-law, Keith Paisley.

'Freddie was very different when I first knew him,' said Staffell, who frequently went round to the house in Feltham where Freddie lived with his parents, Mr and Mrs Bulsara, and his sister, Kashmira.

'The whole family seemed to be very conscious of the fact that they were immigrants, and they seemed to think that there were barriers against them that just didn't exist,' says Staffell, who was surprised when I told him that according to all Queen's publicity material Freddie had been born in Zanzibar and brought up in India.

'He never told me that,' said Staffell, who was at college with Freddie for four years. 'He used to tell me that his family were Persian, but he was always rather reserved when talking about his background ... to this day, I couldn't tell you where he went to school. Although we saw each other practically every day and then later when he got to know Brian we discovered that Brian lived only about a hundred yards away from Freddie, I never heard him say where he'd been educated before going to Ealing.

'During the college holidays, I often used to go round to his house because we became good friends but his parents were always very reserved. His father was then working in the accounts department for Forte's, the catering firm, and I think his mother was working as well ... but it was almost impossible to engage them in conversation. I used to try quite often, but it was as much as they could do to ask me whether I wanted one lump of sugar or two in my tea – the conversations that I had with them were as restricted as that, and I got the impression that they were over-conscious of the immigrant situation in which they found themselves. They were shy people, and I just formed this feeling – which may have been quite wrong – that people were against them because of their background.

'When Jimi Hendrix started, Freddie absolutely idolised him. Hendrix was his God. At college, he used to spend a great deal of his time drawing pictures of Hendrix and I can remember him miming in the art room, holding a twelve-inch ruler as though it were a microphone, and throwing back his head as he mimed the songs. Hendrix was everything to him,

31

and I suspected that it ran a great deal deeper than just the music. Hendrix was the Negro from the ghetto who had pulled himself up by his boot straps and had become totally accepted by everyone, white and black, because of the quality of his music. And although Freddie wasn't impoverished and living in a ghetto, I think now, looking back, that Hendrix represented something to him, a goal that he could achieve himself . . . and I admire Freddie for what he's done since. He's worked enormously hard, and really has pulled himself until now he's a superstar.

'When I first knew him at college, those sort of ideas hadn't started to form – and it was an interesting experience seeing them all take shape as Freddie found himself and discovered what he wanted to do with his life.

'I can remember him in the early days at the college wearing dark grey jackets, it may have been a suit, even, with those old-fashioned Bri-nylon shirts with the tiny collars and a thin little tie. Then we started going round together, and he'd come along with me when I went off on gigs with Smile and he'd stand there at the back or at the side of the stage listening to us play, though he never came up on stage himself at all but he was starting to get interested in the music. That was obvious.'

When Brian May put that advertisement up on the Imperial College board, he met Roger Meddows Taylor, and then with Staffell, they formed a trio, calling themselves Smile. Throughout the four years that they stayed together, they always remained just a trio.

'We were featuring more of our own material now, and because we had Brian on lead and Roger on drums I decided to take up the bass guitar, although I can't clearly remember how or why that came about,' said Staffell. 'I bought a cheap Vox copy of a Fender Precision for thirty pounds, second hand, and then spent the first day sawing the tail-piece down so that it looked like a real Fender. Freddie used to come along and hear us rehearse, and it was interesting to see how his mind developed. Gradually, he started getting more and more interested in the music that we were playing and we started travelling farther afield to gigs, often Freddie came with us because by now he was a friend of the whole group.

'We started to get bookings through an agent, a guy called Marcus, who had a little agency called Rondo in Kensington High Street in the same building as a firm that ran mobile discos called Juliana's Discotheques for whom I used to do some graphics. Then we needed to have our own roadie and got ourselves a tiny green Ford Thames Van and another guy who was at Hampton Grammar School, Pete Edmunds, came along and drove us around as our roadie. He later went on to work for Paul McCartney and Wings.

'As well as playing at little colleges in the London area, occasionally we used to go down to Truro, where Roger was able to arrange for us to play at a club called PJ's, where we built up quite a following . . . there always used to be advertisements in the local paper a week in advance saying "From London – Smile" and then there would be posters outside the club as well, and the place used to get packed out.

'Once we were driving down there for a gig and were due to be paid twenty-five quid, which was just about enough to cover our expenses going down there, leaving about a pound each for us when everything had been paid, like petrol and so on – and then when we got to Andover, the engine seized up. And that put us in a quandary. We didn't know whether to blow out the gig – but instead we phoned one of those firms that provide vans and drivers for musicians and their equipment, and they sent down a van and a bloke who drove us down to Truro for a fee of just twenty-five pounds, which meant that all the money had gone before we had even started to play . . . and he just turned straight round and drove back to London, which meant that we were stranded in Truro with our equipment. In the end, Brian and I caught the Cornish Riviera express back to London, with all our guitars, drums and amplifying equipment in the guard's van, and when we got back to Paddington we walked straight through the barrier with all the gear on a trolley without anyone ever asking to pay any extra. Richard Thompson, the drummer who had been in 1984, picked us up at the station.

33

He was another of the people that we always kept in touch with.

'Those weekends in Cornwall were highlights of our time with Smile because everyone used to make such a fuss of us down there. Pat and Sue Johnstone, who now run the Queen Fan Club, were living down there on and off and they used to let us crash down on their floor sometimes . . . and then other weekends we'd actually get beds to sleep in, and Roger's mother would put us up at her house, which was right in the centre of Truro. Sometimes we'd make a stay of it and play at other venues apart from PJ's like the Flamingo ballroom in Redruth.

'Freddie used to come down to Cornwall with us sometimes, and it always became a great social thing with lots of drinking sessions . . . it was all so much more relaxed down there than in London, and everyone was so kind, inviting us into their homes and to parties and so on.

'Musically, Smile was changing just as every group had changed following Hendrix and Cream. We were attempting to write our own songs, although we were still a bit shaky in those days. Our act included different material to the stuff we'd done in 1984, although we'd still bring that in sometimes, we used to do a heavy rock version of "If I Were A Carpenter" and then a rather creepy version of "Mony Mony", which had been a hit for Tommy James and The Shondells and a song that the British group The Birds had released "How Can It Be", for by then Brian was really blossoming forth as a guitarist. Musically I was the weak link in that band because I'd always been a singer until I took up the bass whereas Brian and Roger had both been playing for years, and Roger had a growing reputation as a drummer among the smaller groups that were around at that time.

'By now, Freddie was sharing a flat in Shepherd's Bush with Roger and then they started running that stall of theirs in Kensington Market, and Freddie was changing considerably although he had still never been a member of a group himself. It was about that time that we signed our recording contract

34

with Mercury/America after meeting Lou Reizner one night when we were doing a gig down at the Speakeasy, or somewhere like that.'

Reizner, whom I interviewed for my book on Rod Stewart in this series, was to prove an important figure in late sixties British rock music. An American producer, he had settled in London and was then running the US company, Mercury's operation in this country. It was he who introduced David Bowie to his wife Angie and who also helped to promote Bowie's first hit single 'Space Oddity', and around the same time he also signed Rod Stewart to his first album contract, producing his first two solo LPs.

He also suggested that Smile should begin recording and arranged for them to go into the Trident studios and cut their first two tracks, 'Earth' (which was written by Tim Staffell) and 'Step On Me' (written by Brian May and Staffell). The tracks were released as a single in the United States and Staffell has one of the original promotion copies, which he showed me while we were talking.

'All that I ever got for that record was a cheque for £1.10p – and we never actually saw it in the shops,' he said. 'It was never released in this country. I think that was because the operation that Mercury had going in London closed down some time afterwards and Lou Reizner went back to the States for a while, though he came back to Britain to do the *Tommy* album. When I went to the States a few years ago I went into a record store just to make sure that it had been released, and the guy behind the counter looked it up in the catalogues, and sure enough, there it was, but I don't think any of us ever saw an actual copy of the single apart from that promotional copy that I've got, which is cracked right down the middle and useless to anyone but me. There may be a pile of them somewhere in the States, stacked away in some warehouse or they may have been pressed down into ash trays. I've got no idea what happened.'

Those two tracks were produced for Mercury by John Anthony, whom Staffell describes as 'a good mate who was always looning around'. It was Anthony who later introduced Queen to Trident Audio Productions (see Chapters Four and Five), and he also has now gone to the States where he is producing the work of another British band, Ace.

'Some time after that we also did another session for Mercury at the De Lane Lea studios,' says Staffell. 'Then we worked with another producer, Fritz Fryer, who had been with the group, The Four Pennies, who had a big hit in Britain with the single "Juliet". We cut four tracks with him, one of those was "Doing All Right", which I wrote with Brian and which Queen later used on their first album. And I think two of the other tracks were "If I Were A Carpenter" and "Mony Mony", although I couldn't be sure after all this time . . . none of that material was ever released and I have no idea what happened to the tapes.

'It was shortly after that that the group broke up. Things had always been so slow with Smile and the group existed under tension – it was just tension that kept the group going, and we were always having arguments about musical direction . . . the only other big thing that we did with Smile was when we appeared at the Albert Hall in a charity show that was organised by Imperial College. It was a big concert with The Bonzo Dog Doo Dah Band, Sue and Sunny, Joe Cocker and Spooky Tooth as well as Free, and we were the first band on in the second half. I'll always remember that because John Peel introduced, and then we all ran out on stage and as I started to sing I pulled out my microphone lead and it all went dead and we had to start again. We started off with our version of "If I Were A Carpenter", something that we were very pleased with, and then went on to "Earth", "Mony Mony" and "See What A Fool I've Been", which is an old blues number that I first heard on a Sonny Terry and Brownie McGhee album. The hall wasn't packed out that night but it was still a great experience to go on stage and look out into an auditorium as large as that – it was the first time that any of us had ever played anywhere like that.

'There's something else that I also remember about that gig, and that was that before it happened we had been talking about expanding the group from a trio into a four-piece group, and we'd been thinking of adding an electric piano, and we had this guy Chris who was going to play with us . . . we'd rehearsed together and played once or twice, but it hadn't worked out – so we blew him out just before the gig, which was a terrible thing to do to him, really, but it was a decision that had to be taken. It was just something that had to be done. After that there was another guy called Phil, who also played piano with us temporarily, but that didn't work out, either, and by then there were rows going on within the group. We were trying to change direction, which was obvious from the way we were trying out different people and seeing what a four-piece combination sounded like . . .'

It was at that point that Staffell left Smile, having by then been associated with Brian May for seven years and Roger Taylor for three. Staffell answered an advertisement for a singer in one of the music papers and thus found himself joining a group with the unlikely name of Humpy Bong that was being formed by Colin Petersen. Petersen had previously been in the Bee Gees, a group that had come over from Australia and had number one hits in Britain, the United States and Europe with singles like 'Massachusetts' and 'New York Mining Disaster'. Also recruited for that group was the singer Jonathan Kelly, who has since pursued his own solo career.

'We thought it was all going to happen because the Bee Gees had been so successful that Petersen only had to walk into record company offices and people would start pulling their cheque books out, but it all came to nothing. Another guy in that band was Peter Wood, who is now with the Sutherland Brothers and Quiver . . . and we did a couple of appearances on "Top Of The Pops", but the band never really got off the ground,' said Staffell.

By then, Mercury – who had been accompanying Smile to so many of their gigs – had made his first stage appearances. A group had come down from Liverpool called Ibex, and then when Smile broke up Freddie became their singer, with the

37

group changing their name to Wreckage. They only worked intermittently because most of the band were still Liverpool-based. Richard Thompson, who had been the drummer in 1984 years earlier, also came back into the picture, playing occasional gigs with Wreckage. And there was another member called 'Miffer' to his friends, who had a milk round in Liverpool and found it hard to decide whether to continue as a musician or carry on delivering milk.

'I had left Smile in the summer of 1970,' said Staffell. 'By then Freddie had left college and was dividing his time between the Kensington Market and doing occasional graphic design jobs . . . he was on the books of an agency in Chancery Lane called Austin Knights, and they actually got him one job as an illustrator for a children's story. It was a space story, but whether Freddie finished it or not, I don't know . . . I never saw any final result.'

Also represented by Austin Knights was another former student from Ealing College of Art, Clive Armitage, who had been in the same class as Staffell and Freddie Mercury and whom I met quite by accident; he called round to see Staffell while we were mid-conversation. And it just so happened that he was one of the few people who ever saw Freddie performing with that short-lived first group Wreckage.

'They did one gig at the Ealing College of Art,' said Armitage. 'There was a guy called John Taylor on bass, who later became road manager for Patto; a guitarist called Mick; this guy Miffer who was playing drums that night instead of Richard Thompson, and Freddie . . . they were wearing those Grandad-style tie-dyed T-shirts and jeans and were singing blues-style songs, very Hendrix-style, heavy blues. Wreckage can't have lasted much more than a year, but even then Freddie was talking of becoming a star. He really did want to be a superstar. That was his ambition, and he was now becoming much more flamboyant in his dress and his whole appearance, and he used to tell people: "I am not going to become a star – I am going to be a legend!" And he said that over and over again. And it wasn't just a boast. HE really believed now that

38

he could do it, and that success would come to him on his own terms . . . he had tremendous determination.'

Like Staffell, Armitage agreed that when Freddie Mercury had first gone to Ealing College of Art as Freddie Bulsara he had been quiet and somewhat shy and retiring. 'I don't think he ever struck me as being particularly positive – and then he became interested in music and he became very positive,' said Staffell, with Armitage nodding his agreement.

'I think the first sign that any of us had that he was getting interested in music was when me and Freddie and another guy called Nigel Foster used to go downstairs to the men's loo at the Ealing College, and we'd sing three-part harmonies which would sound great because the acoustics were terrific, and the sound would go echoing round the building . . . and then later when he bought himself his first guitar, I re-fretted it for him so that he could get a better sound – and it was obvious then that music was awakening something in him . . . he was beginning to cultivate a self-image, although it was not so much vanity as an expression of confidence in his own ability . . . and he was still practising all these poses that he was to use later on stage with Queen.'

Armitage, who had also seen Freddie in the days when he used to demonstrate his Hendrix-poses with the aid of a twelve-inch ruler as a microphone-substitute, saw this development carried a stage further that night that Wreckage appeared at Ealing College of Art.

'When he did a guitar number, he would hold the guitar like this,' said Armitage, his hands at an angle so that one could imagine a guitar held firmly across Mercury's chest. 'And then he used to throw back his head just as he does now with Queen – and it was a very proud gesture . . . he was practising it all the time with Wreckage, and he was obviously becoming a showman. I can remember him saying to Miffer after the show that night: "We must have *an act!*" He was developing routines of his own as a singer, and it was obvious that he wanted to be Somebody, and that his music now was an expression of himself that ran very deep, with the other members of Wreckage being just passengers.

'Freddie was beginning to develop this slightly camp appearance. At the art college he had started wearing very tight trousers with fancy belts, and now he was turning to clothes that were all black, and it seemed to me that in his stage movements he was modelling himself on Robert Plant of Led Zeppelin, although that may have been sub-conscious – everyone had started modelling themselves on Plant, often without even knowing it – you can see bits of Plant in Roger Daltry as The Who developed their act.

'Freddie had now gone through a whole transition; when he first started at the Market he dressed the same as everyone else did . . . but now he was wearing those velvet jackets, tight trousers, long black hair, silver jewellery, with black nail varnish – he was totally Kensington Market. And in his personality he had become much more out-going socially, although when I've seen him recently he's become much more withdrawn again . . . I saw him recently and while we were talking I said: "You are successful, and I am not!" And he just said: "You have only got to do it." And I think that's right; his success is the story of one man being totally determined . . .'

After Staffell had left Smile in 1970, Mercury eventually quit the other group Wreckage and then he became the singer in Staffell's place, although Mercury, May and Taylor changed the name to Queen. Their total image was something that had been developing in Mercury's mind while he worked away in the Market selling old clothes and suede boots. For a long time, almost certainly longer than a year, there was just the three of them – although they did work with a succession of different bass guitarists before they eventually recruited John Deacon, whom they had first seen playing with another group in a Chelsea disco. When he answered an advertisement, they offered him the job.

Like Roger Taylor, Deacon was another student from the provinces who had come to London in pursuit of a career. He had been born in Leicester, going first to the Oadby Infant

School, then Gartree High School and on to Beauchamp Grammar School, where he got the necessary O-levels and A-levels to win a place at Chelsea College (which is part of London University), where he wanted to study electronics. Deacon had started playing with local groups in Leicester when he was fourteen, starting with one called Opposition, which played all the local youth clubs and village halls, and then moving on to another called Art. He, too, had been influenced by Hendrix and Cream – but when he moved down to London to start studying for his degree his bass guitar and amplification equipment was left behind at his mother's home in Oadby. (His father died when he was younger.) 'I packed up groups for a while,' he has said since. After gaining that science degree he indeed went on to become a teacher in a comprehensive school, a job he kept for four years until Queen became fully professional around the time of the *Queen II* album.

Tim Staffell first saw Queen as they are today with Deacon as the fourth member of the group at a rugby club New Year's Eve dance at the end of December 1971. 'Brian was then still at Imperial College, Roger was at the North London Polytechnic, and John was still teaching but Freddie was still down at Kensington Market, and he was starting to write like crazy,' said Staffell.

'I saw them play that night, and then had a long chat with them afterwards. They didn't have very much gear, but a friend of theirs John Harris was acting as their roadie – and he's still with them today – and I noticed that their stage act had changed considerably. They were now including more and more of their own material, and I thought perhaps they might be thinking of recording but Brian told me that he was still slightly frightened of the ogres of the music business. He had always been very worried about the possibility of signing contracts and what that might mean, and it was something that hadn't left him. He told me that he was now reading for his doctorate at Imperial, and he was anxious to complete that before committing himself full-time to music.

'They were working intermittently by then, but not at all

the usual places; they'd get booked into tiny colleges tucked away in odd places so that they were developing without people really being very aware of them as a group, although I think that was purely an accident.

'On stage that night, they featured "Stone Cold Crazy", which is the number with the very fast sequence which Freddie sings at high speed and which they later used on the third album along with "Liar", "See What A Fool I've Been" and their rock medley, which included "Jailhouse Rock"; and they were starting to get a really coherent act together . . . Freddie was now much more extroverted than he had ever been, and had developed this strong personality that he has now, with the forceful movements with the microphone and throwing his head back as he strode forward – although there wasn't much room for him to move that night at the rugby club because Queen were down on the floor with people dancing all around them. I don't think Freddie has ever been through periods of self-consciousness in all the years that I had known him, but that night it was clear that he was finding something himself through music. I think it's the music and the market that did everything for him – he always had had a lot of style even at Ealing College of Art, but it was joining with the people in the group and working in Kensington Market that drew all that out of them, and looking back now it was fascinating to see the way it all developed. I don't think he ever had any doubt that he would eventually be somebody.'

CHAPTER THREE

When Queen's first single 'Keep Yourself Alive' and their first album, 'Queen' were released in July 1973, the initial reaction of the press was sceptical. It was nearly the end of the 'Glam Rock' era – and there was a general feeling abroad that Queen were just another fey camp act trying to jump aboard the David Bowie–Gary Glitter–Marc Bolan–Sweet–Slade band-waggon.

The impression was not helped when it was learned that Queen's lead singer, Freddie Mercury, was none other than the mysterious Larry Lurex whose first single had been released only a few weeks earlier – but as very few copies had ever been sold of the Lurex single it was the name that caused the doubts, not the music.

I have a copy of that single, 'I Can Hear Music' (written by Greenwich, Spector and Barry) coupled with 'Goin' Back', a Goffin-King song which had once been recorded by Dusty Springfield. The tracks were produced by Robin Geoffrey Cable, and this, too, was described as a 'Trident Audio Pro-duction'. It is nothing to be ashamed of, though different in style to Queen's later work, for Freddie's voice still has that slight lisping sound on his 's's' and Brian May's guitar work and Roger Taylor's drumming combine effectively enough, but more in a Phil Spector sort of way than in the style we now associate with Queen. Those piercing, pure guitar solos are absent; instead, there's a wall-of-sound guitar effect that re-minds one of some of the early backings to the Righteous Brothers.

Just why the Larry Lurex single was ever released under that name remains an almost total mystery; something that Mercury himself has never explained – and which Norman Sheffield and Dave Thomas of Trident simply refer to as a 'jokey sort of thing that we did for fun'. There was no attempt to launch a new Gary Glitter sort of pop star – even though that is what the name itself suggests.

Anyway, the record did not happen, and so they issued hardly any press material. There are no embarrassing photographs of Mr Lurex floating around. Only the music remains, and if you do get the chance do listen to it because the single shows another aspect of May's work as a guitarist – and "I Can Hear Music" always was a good song!

Less than a month after the Larry Lurex single, Queen themselves released their first single and then a week later the 'Queen' album. The reviews of the single, Brian May's 'Keep Yourself Alive', were varied. This is what was said:

> 'If these guys look half as good as they sound, they could be huge. But that name threatens more Roxy/Bowie/Sweet gay games, which not only wind up distracting the musicians from playing music, but are going out-of-fashion. The sound goes back past Roxy to the Who and the Electric Prunes, using moog as music, not just sound effects, managing to make the scattershot lyrics mean something. Good singer, cleanly recorded. Do us all a favour, fellers, change your name to the Uncouth and go on stage in jock-straps.'
>
> – *New Musical Express*

> 'A raucous, but still well-built single. The vocal interchanges make it stand out in a rather crowded week. Good power from behind, but the vocal depths make it.'
>
> – *Record Mirror*

> 'Here's a band they keep talking about, and they make an impressive debut with a heavily phased guitar intro and energetic vocal attack. But the tune lacks originality, and I don't think this one will be a hit.'
>
> – *Melody Maker*

> 'Queen's PR, a solid young hipster, hastens to add that Queen are a minor sensation, stunningly visual, etc. Doubt-

44

less, they're kind to their parents and dumb animals too; beneath those shiny showbiz exteriors they're regular guys (former scouts and graduate meals-on-wheels moguls). This genteel refrain kicks off (a popular expression dans le business) with a scrubbing, phased rhythm guitar, joined by an attractively stilted, vaguely Hendrix-y lead riff merging into the body (or outer casing) of the tune, a tromping, chordy, early Who-style passage with frantic white-boy vocals, and a drum solo that'd make Dave Clark's day. It should do well.'

– *Disc*

'Queen have already been heard on my Thursday night "Sound Of The 70's". (You remember, the one you never miss.) They were pretty positive there, heavy, but not totally predictable like so many of their brethren. This single is sort of odd really. I suspect they've tried to do so many things to keep it out of the rut but in so doing they've driven the whole charabanc off the road and into the ditch. It opens with some medium weirdness, phased strumming and so on, lashes into a boogie with the usual stuff about being a superstar. It's well executed, the voices are very white and there's some pleasing guitar and synthesiser work involved. Nevertheless it never really gets going, the excitement is spurious. A pity. Perhaps next time.'

– Bob Harris, *Sounds*

'This really is one of the best singles of the year, and ought to set the gracious Queen on the road to success. The more I play it, the more I am convinced it has everything a hit single needs – without being overtly commercial. The guitar work is fast, precise and ear-catching, and the vocal refrain will keep coming back and hitting you after the first hearing. Long live Queen.'

– *Birmingham Mail*

'This is a marching, charging band that will soon be making headlines in the sledgehammer and boots variety of rock.

45

Young, beautiful, possessed of demonic rock and roll fire —
what more could a fan craving pin-ups and urging to unleash
total devotion ask for in a group? Nothing of course, and the
hell-fire sounds of Queen could be rocketing from speakers
everywhere before the summer is over.'

— Middlesex Times

'If this debut sound from Queen is anything to go by, they
should make very interesting listening in the future. Clever
use of electronic phasing gives way to a thundering piece of
rock at its best. The sound gallops along at a frightening pace
and includes great drum and guitar breaks. Rating – good.'

— South Yorkshire Times

By the time the single and the album were released, the
material itself was already over twelve months old; Queen had
been continuing with either day-time jobs or their studies
while they waited for Trident to reach a distribution agreement
with one of the major record companies. In the end, the company that did take Queen's material was EMI and in Chapters
Four, Five and Six the personal and financial implications of
all this are told in considerable detail. There were several
crucial stages at which Queen could have disappeared without
trace had someone not intervened, an aspect of a group's success that is seldom told.

Two friends of the group, sisters Pat and Sue Johnstone,
who had grown up in the same Cornish town as Roger Meddows
Taylor, and then later came to London around the same time
to run their own stall in Kensington Market while Freddie and
Roger ran theirs, were brought in to run the Queen Fan Club —
and they are still doing so to this day, being paid a salary by
the group. The press and publicity side was organised by
Trident too, with the account being allocated to one of the top
independent publicists, Tony Brainsby, whose other clients at
the time included Paul McCartney and Cat Stevens. His
assistant at the time was John Bagnall, who — by another odd
coincidence — later became label manager at EMI Records. I

46

interviewed them all while assembling the material for this book.

Initially, Pat and Sue Johnstone were reluctant to talk to me. With Queen changing management and moving to John Reid, they, too, had moved across to Reid's offices, being given a tiny, windowless office in the basement, where they sat each day on opposite sides of a desk, opening fan mail and applications to join the Queen Fan Club from all over the world. Their reluctance was due to the fact that they had agreed to co-operate in writing another book which was due to be published by Brown and Watson, with all the normal royalties being paid into the Queen Fan Club to make it financially independent.

'This is something we're very anxious about,' explained Pat Johnstone, 'because until now the club has been run on a shoestring. When we were asked to help with the writing of that book, the people here arranged for it to be done to help the Club.'

The Johnstone sisters were brought up near Truro, which was where Roger Meddows Taylor went to school. 'We used to know him at that time because he was in a local group called Reaction, and I was singing in a folk club,' said Sue. The sisters were also friends of the girlfriend that Roger was going out with at the time. 'We were all involved in music down there, and kept bumping into each other all the time,' said Pat.

Around the same time that Roger moved to London to begin a course at the London School of Dentistry, which he abandoned after only a year's study, Pat also left Cornwall and settled in London, initially working as a nanny and then also taking a stall in Kensington Market where Roger had his stall with Freddie Mercury. A year after Pat had left home, with her group Wizard breaking up, Sue also moved to London.

'Roger was then playing in Smile, and we all used to travel back to Cornwall occasionally because he was able to set up bookings for the group down there – and then later when Queen was formed, they, too, used to travel down to Cornwall sometimes,' said Pat. 'Freddie had got to know Brian and Roger through the Kensington Market, and was always going around

47

with them, going along to their gigs even before Queen was formed. They weren't doing much at all in those days, just a few college gigs – and then when there was just the three of them, they really needed a bass player and that was when John Deacon joined them. They had seen him playing at some disco in Chelsea, and then later he answered an advertisement and because they knew him they asked him to join the group. This went on for a year or so before they signed with Trident, and they spent a lot of time putting down tapes of songs they'd written. Freddie had finished at the Ealing College of Art, and had trained as an illustrator and graphic designer and he had all sorts of artistic ideas for their clothes and general appearance on stage, and it was all sort of fusing together. There was a great atmosphere in the Market in those days; we were all involved in it together and it was work and social life all combined. We'd be running our stalls during the day, and then we'd all go off to the pub together in the evenings before going off to concerts. Every night, people would be saying "Which concert are you going to?", there was a coming-together of musicians and artists who all had something in common through the market. And the thing that brought Roger, Freddie and Brian together was that they were all total Hendrix freaks. He was their hero at the time. John Harris, who went on to become their sound engineer, was involved with them too because his girlfriend was at college with Brian's girlfriend. Everyone was sort of mingling together, and Jimi Hendrix's music was the thing that they all used to share and talk about.'

After dropping out of that dentistry course, Roger went on to study biology at the North London Polytechnic and then at the laboratories at Kew Gardens, where he also studied botany; for a while he kept on his stall with Freddie Mercury, and then Mercury stayed on at the market, helping another friend, Alan Mair.

And when, after all the delays while Trident sorted out the business side, Queen finally started promoting their single and their album, Pat and Sue Johnstone were brought in to run the Fan Club. It took a while to get started. To begin with, as letters were starting to come in from fans who had seen them on their early dates just after the first album and then later on the Mott the Hoople tour, Pat and Sue would send back a typed letter from the Trident offices explaining that Queen were now working on their second LP; that 'The Seven Seas of Rhye' was to be released as a single; that they were planning a tour of their own – and that fans could join the club for 50 pence a year. 'In return for this vast sum you will receive the usual goodies, such as news-sheets, special T-shirts, badges, stickers and posters, etc,' they wrote.

It was all fairly amateurish compared with the detailed planning that went into the organisation of fan clubs such as those for fans of the Osmonds and Slade. But eventually, they got their stocks of membership cards, printed in gold on a black background with the 'Queen' motif that Freddie Mercury had designed for the group, incorporating each of their zodiac signs. And they got their stationery, again with the 'Queen' motif and stocks of stickers priced at forty pence, transfers at thirty pence and posters for forty pence. Periodically, each member of the group would prepare a hand-written letter and this would be reproduced and distributed to the members along with details of concert tours, record releases, visits overseas, and details of new merchandise.

For instance, at Christmas-time 1975, Freddie Mercury wrote the seasonal message to the fans that began: 'Hello Dears . . .' and ended, '. . . have an outrageous Christmas and a naughty New Year – love and kisses to all you darlings, Freddie.' As far as these fan clubs can be, it was all friendly and personal – though you still had to pay £3.50 for a sweat shirt with the motif from the album sleeve of *A Night At The Opera*.

'We're trying to make the club as fully self-supporting financially as we can,' explained Pat and Sue Johnstone, which should not be too difficult now that it has around 10,000 members in this country and Europe, with another 7,000 members in a separate fan club in Japan.

Although maybe not quite so close to the group now as they

were in the Kensington Market days because their success takes Queen to far-flung places, Pat and Sue continue to run the club, answering the thousands of letters that come flowing in. 'We're lucky – because we've been able to watch the group develop through every stage of their career,' say the Johnstone sisters, who feel – as do so many of the people associated with Queen – that the group's success really started with the concert they gave at the Imperial College in Kensington at the beginning of November, 1973, after they had finished recording their second album and were rehearsing for their tour with Mott the Hoople, which opened a few days later.

Another person who was there that night was Alan Mair, who had also had a stall at the Kensington Market. Mair, who still lives in London, had originally come down from Glasgow as the bass player of the Scottish group, The Beatstalkers, who had moved down south in the mid-sixties, had seven singles released by Decca – but eventually broke up having failed to make their break-through.

When The Beatstalkers split, Mair took the market stall, selling suede boots and trousers which he had people making for him in his own workshop in North London.

'I had my boot stall for four years, and to begin with Roger and Freddie had another stall of their own. Then after the group had signed with Trident, Roger ceased coming to the market and Freddie worked with me on my stall for eighteen months or so,' said Mair. 'It was always a very casual sort of relationship; when I couldn't come into the Market some days, Freddie would look after my stall for me and I'd pay him a couple of pounds, or something like that, there was never much money in it. He wasn't really working at building up his stall by then because his intention was to turn fully professional as soon as the group were able to. He was a very pleasant, inoffensive sort of person, and the thing I admire about Freddie now looking back on that period was that even though he knew that I'd worked in a group he never tried to force his own ideas on anyone. Until Queen started and I first saw them play, none of us in the Market had any idea of their musical talents – and in all the time he worked with me he never told me how good he was or what he wanted to do professionally. He just used to say, "We've got this little band together."

'I went to the very first gig that Queen ever did, which must have been about four years ago; they appeared one night at the Estates Management Hall, which was round the back of the market, and there were about two hundred people there, mostly people who had heard of them through the market – and they were terrible. They were badly out of tune that night, and believe it or not most people who saw them that night were saying afterwards that they didn't seem to have much going for them.

'Being a musician myself, I thought they were very bad because there was a certain lack of finesse about their act. They were very raw. It was their very first show together, and Freddie's voice was very uncontrolled, and he was also stiff in his movements on stage, sort of cumbersome . . . he came on dressed in all black with velvet trousers and a jacket, but I can't remember what the others were wearing at all. They seemed rather nondescript. Even then, it was Freddie who was the dresser; he used to walk around the market during the day-time wearing black nail-polish; and all they had was those small fifty-watt amplifiers.

'Freddie didn't talk very much about what they were planning to do, and then one day he came in to work on the stall and told me: "We will probably be turning professional." But he said he'd need to carry on working down the market a little bit longer until the money started coming in, and in the end he carried on working on my stall for it must have been a good twelve months more after that. It probably took them a year before they started to get into their stride, and then after "Seven Seas of Rhye" he stopped coming down, though he still drops in now and again down at the Greyhound pub, which was where we all used to go every night after we'd closed up our stalls.

'Freddie was always easy-going and quiet, and would never say anything to offend anyone. I don't think he is capable of being harmful to anyone who hasn't been harmful to him; he always seemed so mellow – and I never saw him lose his temper all the time I knew him . . . he used to have a flat in Holland Park then, the same flat that he's got now, and he lived there with his girlfriend, Mary Austin. I don't know how they met, but they've been together five years now, and were always quite inseparable when he was down at the market. She was on the managerial staff at Biba's, and when they closed each night she'd come round to the market, which was only a few doors away, and then we'd all go round to the Greyhound, where Freddie would prop himself up against the bar, always drinking Tequila Sunrise or a cocktail. He always used to have this sort of presence, even then, he was tall and slim, always dressed in black with his long black hair and his black-painted nails, and from a woman's point of view he was a very attractive guy. The girls in the market would talk about him, saying "Can't you imagine what he would look like on stage?" But the boys in the market didn't think of him as any sort of sex symbol, and I never saw him going around with any other girl but Mary.

'He never talked very much about his background, and I was the kind of person who wouldn't think to ask. I always had the impression that he was very single-minded. Music is like that; if you're a musician you tend to be only interested in your music or in talking to other musicians who understand what you're saying. Although we saw each other nearly every day for four years and Freddie spent eighteen months actually working on my stall I never even knew that he read music or could play piano until Queen played that gig at the Imperial College.

'He had a very good way of talking to customers, and could usually persuade them to pay thirteen pounds a pair for the boots and no matter who came along he'd handle it all very coolly. That was really the impression that I had of him until Imperial College, which was quite an amazing gig. Later I saw them at the Rainbow, and then again at the Hammersmith Odeon this last Christmas, when Freddie left me a couple of tickets for the show. After the gig, I went backstage to see him and Mary was there – and he was still just the same as he'd been back in the market days. I think that was the most amazing thing of all, really, he'd developed the style that he has now long before it all happened.

'Everyone who ever worked at the market was influenced by the whole era. You worked together and you shared the same social life, and a lot of people all grew up the same way. It would be unfair to say that Freddie was the exception, everyone was influenced by the market, but I think it was while he was working there that Freddie developed his sense of style. What we didn't realise was that there was a very strong-willed personality developing underneath all this as well. None of us knew of the writing that he was doing, although I'd heard him sing "Liar" at that very first concert they did – but we didn't know how much thought was going into everything they did, and how unusual their music really was. He was heading somewhere, but it didn't show.'

Even while he was popping in and out of the market, earning the odd few pounds helping out on Alan Mair's stall, Mercury and the other members of Queen had signed with Trident; a year had gone by while Trident negotiated with different companies before setting up that distribution agreement with EMI, and as the autumn of 1973 approached and the group completed work on their second album, Queen themselves were anxious to have a stage act that was bold and exciting. And they also needed publicity so that their ideas could become known to a wider audience – which was where Tony Brainsby and his then assistant John Bagnall came in.

'I was asked to represent the group by Jack Nelson, who was then head of Trident, and who invited me round to their offices, where he played me their first album,' said Brainsby. 'It seemed to me that Queen were an interesting group, and I liked working with EMI because every time they'd been associated with a group that I'd been handling I'd always had the closest co-operation with the record company. They always get behind their artists.

'Initially, it was difficult ... some of the teeny papers

started writing about them even though they hadn't had a hit record because the group looked good, and this story about their degrees and the Kensington Market and Brian May being an infra-red astronomer was something that they could all get their teeth into. The music papers started to get a bit interested with the first album, although they tended to slag them off at first writing about them as though they were phoney. They called it "supermarket rock" and described them as a "contrived band" – and that was something that we had to overcome, that the group themselves never really forget. It really hurt them.

'They were a new band and so they were that bit more sensitive to what the critics had to say than musicians who have been around a little longer; a more mature band would have read the critics without letting it affect them . . . after the second album, the music papers were on their side a little more.

'I went to one of their first gigs, which was really just something to help them get their act together. It was down at a little college in Surrey; I can't remember where it was now . . . it was one of those sort of gigs where groups of boys were standing round the bar saying "Let's pull old Mary from the Lower Sixth!" They were raw, but it was a good set – you could see that there was something there. And then, of course, it all started to happen when they went out on that tour with Mott the Hoople. We were representing Mott at the same time so we saw a lot of them on that tour.

'Right from the word go the strange thing about Queen was that they knew exactly what they wanted. They were a very strong-minded group. The first time they came into my office, they produced a sheaf of polaroid pictures that they'd taken themselves and said, "Those are our publicity pictures." And they were different to the sort of pictures I usually had to distribute: groups posed with bowls of flowers, ornamental backgrounds and subdued lighting . . . pictorially, they knew just what they were after and what kind of image they wanted to project. And that's an unusual quality to find in a new band.

'I worked closely with them after that because the secret of being a good publicist isn't in inventing things but in projecting what is really there – and Queen knew that they had something to project. It was as simple as that, really; all we had to do was help them project it.'

The first interview that Brainsby arranged for any member of the group was that one with the magazine *Guitar* (which I quoted briefly in the first chapter) to whom Brian May explained how he had built his own guitar, allowing the magazine to reproduce several of the photographs he had taken in his teens showing the different sections of the guitar on his father's workbench as he was assembling it.

'The only total resistance that I had was from one well-known writer on one of the music papers who told me bluntly that he "wasn't going to write about a load of poofters" – but apart from that we gradually started setting up interviews with all the right people,' said Brainsby.

'Pictorially, the group had very strong ideas of their own; after bringing in those polaroid photos of their own, which really weren't suitable for newspaper reproduction, they always used the same photographer, Mick Rock. And it was always well controlled by the group themselves. He would take lots of photographs of them, and then they would go through the whole lot, rejecting picture after picture until there would be just one or two left – and then I'd be given copies of that to distribute. And they'd stick to their guns over something like that. They thought photographs were important, and you wouldn't be able to persuade them to issue any photos other than those that they'd agreed. They're very strong people; it's totally ingrained in them . . .'

Apart from that sort of image-projection, and the way newspapers all round the world seized on the unusual academic background that the group had, the other story that was seized upon by the press during the period up to and beyond the release of their third album, *Sheer Heart Attack*, was the slightly camp, almost bi-sexual appearance that Freddie Mercury seemed to be cultivating. In fact, no one could be more heterosexual than Mercury who had been living with his girlfriend

Mary Austin at their flat in Holland Park since the very beginning of his days at Kensington Market – but he went along with the press, calling them 'My dears' and 'Darling', and flicking his wrist rather limply.

'I think that was something that developed more or less accidentally, and it did get a little out of hand – but the fact that they called themselves "Queen" obviously had something to do with it, although they always went to great lengths to say the name had been chosen because of its regal connotations. The other thing about Freddie was that he was quite self-conscious about his mouth, and if you look through the photographs that were issued you'll notice that in nearly every one he has his mouth closed.'

Brainsby handled Queen's publicity right through the period from the release of the single 'Keep Yourself Alive' and the album *Queen*, through the Mott the Hoople tour, the second and third albums, the hit singles 'The Seven Seas of Rhye' and 'Killer Queen', until September 1975, when the group had switched from Trident to John Reid's management. 'We still carried on representing them for a few weeks after they'd gone to John Reid, and then quite out of the blue one Friday afternoon a letter was delivered to me saying that my services were being dispensed with "as of now", and that in future Queen's publicity would be handled by the Rocket press office,' said Brainsby.

'It came as a great surprise, though losing accounts is something you have to get used to,' said Brainsby, 'though I will say this for the group, that weekend every single member of the group phoned me privately at home, said how sorry he was that we would be no longer working together, and each of them thanked me for what I'd done, and they all explained that it had been a management decision.'

On the wall at his office, Brainsby still has a large framed poster advertising the *Sheer Heart Attack* album, which is signed by each member of the group – 'with kisses – Freddie', 'from the heights of fabdom – Roger', 'love – John Deacon', and 'love and kisses – Brian May'.

56

Having seen them perform so many times, and having worked with them professionally, I asked Brainsby what he thought their future would be. 'I think potentially they're even bigger than Led Zeppelin – they're one of the really great bands that Britain has produced,' he said without hesitation. And he was not talking as their publicist!

When Brainsby first took on the Queen account, his assistant was John Bagnall, who is now the label manager for EMI Records, and thus responsible for much of the promotion arrangements for their current material.

'I was sitting in Tony's office the day they first came in to see us,' said Bagnall. 'And they looked like stars the very first time they walked through the door . . . Freddie came in wearing a blue silk jacket with white trousers, Roger had an embroidered jacket with that long blond hair, and Brian was dressed from head to toe in black velvet, and the effect was sensational, because you must remember that by the summer of 1973 apart from the teenybop bands all the top groups were down to T-shirts and jeans, so it all seemed very surprising, even sensational . . . but it was the way they carried it off that was so effective. There was nothing camp about them at all. The camp thing was just a role that was thrust at Freddie and which he played along with.

'The thing that was so different about them wasn't so much their music, although that was good; the vital ingredient in Queen's make-up was their absolute belief that they would make it . . . I remember seeing them for the first time at the Marquee just before Christmas 1972, when they hadn't even signed with EMI and then some time later in the summer of 1973 I saw them again appearing at a girls' school dance in Basingstoke. It was one of those gigs they did when they were getting their act right, and this was a strange sort of gig – there were about 300 people in this fairly small modern school hall, standing around the buffet with their glasses of orange juice.

'It really was the embryonic Queen stage act that night, and I remember going backstage afterwards and seeing Freddie slumped in their dressing room, physically shattered by the act

57

they'd just gone through and saying that he wasn't fit enough yet and would have to do some exercises. He had virtually lost his voice and was coughing most of the journey back to London, but what I remember most clearly is that as he was changing I saw that his legs were absolutely black with bruises and he explained that that was where he had been slapping his thighs with a tambourine during different numbers . . . I think that was the first time that I ever had a real awareness of how much physical pain and effort could go into such a stage performance.

'Afterwards, as we were driving back to London, we stopped for coffee on the service station along the M3 and I remember speculating about the future with them. I was talking to Brian and it was obvious that they had an utter belief in their ability to achieve success. They were talking about "In two years' time *when* we have made it . . ." not as though it was a possibility, but as a certainty. They had this complete confidence in themselves, and yet there was no arrogance. They had chosen the path they were going to follow with a full awareness of all the pitfalls and the odds against them, and they were determined to be successful.

'The next time I saw them was at that concert at the Imperial College, and by that time word had spread around London that they were an up-and-coming band and that first album of theirs was starting to earn them some recognition. And being a home gig for them, the hall was absolutely packed with maybe 1,400 to 1,500 people there and only about six square inches of room. I watched them from the front, right in front of their PA speakers and it was unbearably hot. By then they had completed their second album but what impressed me was that they were already playing material which they said from the stage would be included in their *third* album. You could see that there was a wealth of original material there, and the reception they had from the audience that night was ecstatic . . . you only had to listen to them that night to know that they *had* to happen, and that musically they just couldn't be ignored.

'And then afterwards I went backstage to see them, and that

was an extraordinary experience in itself because it was like going backstage to see world stars; there was a long queue of people waiting for autographs, and there was the sort of excitement that you usually feel only after a world class band like The Who or The Stones have given a concert. The girls all wanted Freddie to sign their arms and the boys were anxious to talk to Brian about his guitar.

'I remember talking to Roger that night and saying that it had gone so well that I had the feeling they were going to happen now, and him saying to me: "I really feel we're going to make it now. I really feel it's going to happen." And it sounds silly when I say it now, but I told him that I thought he'd probably have to wait until about the following March – why I said the following March, I don't know, because on the face of it that's a very odd thing to have said. It was a funny sort of psychic conviction, but it was the following March that they had their first hit with "The Seven Seas of Rhye" . . .'

The turning-point came just a few days after that concert at Imperial College when Queen began their British tour as the supporting act to Mott the Hoople. Normally, support groups get fairly rough treatment from audiences who have gone along just to see the top-of-the-bill attraction, and very often the bill-topping acts treat their supports badly, allowing them little time for sound-checks. But Mott had been through the mill themselves, and treated Queen generously.

The scene had been set with an ecstatic review of that Imperial College gig by Rosemary Horide in *Disc*:

'SOLD OUT, said the sign on the door. Amazing, that an unknown (or almost) group like Queen should sell out a gig at Imperial College. But having seen them now, I understand why. Six months ago, when I last saw the band, they showed promise but weren't very together. Their leader Freddie Mercury pranced about the small stage, waving his mike both violently and sensually as they performed numbers from their first album: most notable of which were their single "Keep Yourself Alive" and "Son and Daughter".

The atmosphere in the hall was electric. The kids were with Queen all the way, showing a remarkable knowledge of the band's repertoire and greeting each number uproariously.

The group were musically very good, their stage presence was excellent, and when you consider that the material was all their own, it was a remarkable performance for a new group. The material was far above average, and it was obvious how hard the band worked at entertaining by the tremendous rapport that was established.

At the end of the set, after a couple of standard rock 'n' rollers to provide a fitting climax, the audience wouldn't let Queen go. They were forced on stage to do three encores, until they finally had to stop – not from lack of demand, but sheer exhaustion. The funniest moment was undoubtedly the first encore – Freddie's "Big Spender" was done à la Shirley Bassey, and thus was outrageously camp.

On the whole it was a very good night, and a highly creditable performance. If Queen are this good on the tour with Mott the Hoople (which they start next week) Mott had better watch out. Queen could turn out to be a bit more than just a support band.'

That was one of the more far-seeing of all the early pieces written about the group, and proved to be accurate. Their tour with Mott the Hoople was a sensational success – one of the first times that a support group had virtually stolen the show in many years; perhaps not on this scale since The Beatles toured supporting Helen Shapiro back in 1963. At EMI and Trident, reports kept coming in from all over the country of the impact that Queen were having with their stage act, and this soon started to reflect itself in sales of that first album.

In *Disc*, although Mott naturally received the most coverage, it was reported that: 'Mott and Queen like each other and there's none of the usual mistrust between their roadies. "Queen," says Buffin (of Mott) thankfully, "are not a sabotage band and we have had to work with some in the past – roadies who fall over leads pulling them out by accident on purpose." The concert itself is excellent – one of the best I have seen in ages. Queen's peculiar equipment serves them well. Lead singer Freddie Mercury parodies everybody, but has style and gets away with it.'

And then *Sounds* writer Martin Hayman reported:

'But I must single out Queen for praise. They're a good-looking foursome, play a slashing, hard-driving rock and roll with the same right-now feeling as Mott, even with old rockers like "Jailhouse Rock". I understand they have been together for longer than it would seem – two or three years at least, when they were semi-pro and still finishing college – and it shows . . . I predict a good future for Queen.'

Only in the *Melody Maker* was it said:

'Queen were rather disappointing with a chilly, gutless sound that just didn't project itself off stage. No one number was distinctive, except perhaps "Liar".'

By late 1973, all the music papers were fast becoming alerted to the fact that the group was on the verge of the big-time – and Brian May was now telling *Sounds* and *Melody Maker* the stage-by-stage story of how he had constructed his own guitar! By January 1974 – even without them ever having had a hit record – the group were getting full page features. And other members of Queen were explaining that Brian's home-made instrument was so weird and wonderful that he could make it sound like violins or French horns. At the *Sounds* office, the staff were in no doubt – a large headline said that Queen were now: 'BRITAIN'S BIGGEST UNKNOWNS'. This was to some extent confirmed a few days later when in the *Sounds* annual readers' poll, Queen were voted *third* in the Best New Band (British) section and *ninth* in the Best New Band (International) section. And then a few days later in the *Disc* poll, Queen were voted *tenth* in the Brightest Hope for

1974 category – and in the *New Musical Express* poll they were voted *second* Most Promising Name. All of which was a quite extraordinary thing to have happened to a group that had never had a hit single.

Clearly, something was stirring – and each week the letters' columns in the music papers would have a letter or two about Queen from a reader who had seen them on tour with Mott the Hoople, predictions that they were going to be as big as Led Zeppelin or the New York Dolls (!), enquiries about where they were born, bought their clothes or had their homes, or requests for information about their next record releases.

Over in the United States, something similar was happening – to EMI's astonishment they heard that 130,000 copies of the first Queen album had been sold in America without the group ever having visited the country. It had even crept into the lower end of the *Billboard* LP chart.

All they really needed now was a hit record – and that soon came.

On February 25th, EMI released the second Queen single, the Freddie Mercury number 'The Seven Seas of Rhye', which had originally appeared in shortened form on the first album, and which the group had since re-recorded for the *Queen II* LP with some quite stunning guitar-work by Brian May. The album was released just a few days after the single as Queen were about to begin their second tour, this time headlining themselves. Reaction to their new material was very varied:

'Taken from the forthcoming *Queen II* LP and heard recently on my Thursday programme . . . I like Queen for their excess and their craziness although cynical friends have described them as "Sweet gone heavy". By their own standards this single is pretty restrained although there's some crunching guitar to be heard and enjoyed. Piano opens the side and the lyrics seem to concern themselves with some bloke who shuffles in from outer-space to run the show down here. As I understand it he's a pretty easy-going sort of chap – until you cross him and then he jumps on you from a great height. I may have got most of that wrong so don't believe it implicitly. A lot takes place musically as the tale of der-ring-do unfurls, there are some high harmonies that'll give your cat sleepless nights, guitars roar and thunder and a good time is so be had by all. Just as you think the lyrics are be-coming a shade Moody Blues-ish you find that Queen, God bless 'em, have moved somehow into "I Do Like To Be Beside The Seaside". Could even ease its way into the lower reaches. Hope so.'

– Sounds (on single)

'This is it, the dregs of glam rock. The band with the worst name have capped that dubious achievement by bringing out the worst album for some time. Their material is weak and overproduced. The Black Side (literally!) is penned by vocalist Freddie Mercury, while the White Side except for "Loser In The End" are written by guitarist Brian May. That track, written by drummer Roger Taylor, must be the worst piece of dross ever committed to plastic – like "She's Leaving Home" meets Black Sabbath? As a whole it is dire, while the musicianship isn't a lot better. Brian May is techni-cally proficient but Freddie Mercury's poor voice is dressed up with multi-tracking. The rhythm section is fairly good. A lot of people are pushing Queen as the band of '74. If this is our brightest hope for the future then we are committing rock and roll suicide.'

– Record Mirror (on the LP)

'Appreciating that it may take a band at least three or more albums to achieve their potential, Queen seems to cut corners rather hastily to reach recording success, and tend on *Queen II* to misrepresent their current stature. And that is basically the most offensive quality of this album, and frankly an off-putting one. Although "Procession" and "Father To Son" set a promising start to the set, Queen's aura of self-import-ance, the guitar licks running like an interminable nose bleed, the falsetto chorus, doomy chords all are contrived to hide the obvious Who heavy energy rock feel . . . in my opinion there is nothing *that* important on this album which demands such contrived arrangements. Queen are obviously trying to dupe everyone about their own limited abilities. In their defence, their arrangements at times can be excellent and certainly precise. And the compositions of Brian May . . . have that hint of melodic credibility which makes them pleasing . . . to add credibility to their growing reputation, Queen will have to cut this aura of self-laudatory crap, and make a decent album.'

— *New Musical Express* (on the LP)

'With one's favourite group there's a great temptation to eulogise, without being very constructive, critical or informative. So the best I can do to try to be all those things is to give you a run-down of the tracks from Queen's second album . . . to sum up, I'll confine myself to saying that this is the best album from a relatively new group I've ever heard. The material, performance and recording and even artwork standards are very high. And it's going to be a hit album.'

— *Disc* (on the LP)

'Queen have come up with quite an inspiring follow-up to their first and most excellent debut album. Simply titled *Queen II* this album captures them in their finest hours. The music is energetic and Freddie Mercury's vocals soar to grand heights. But alas there are a few disappointments that set back the quality of the album. The production seems shoddy in places and sometimes the numbers are a bit excessive building up to no real climax. But no matter the band have plenty of time to polish themselves . . . Brian May must be the most promising guitarist to have arisen in Britain in recent years. The sheer confidence and power of his playing add to the many dimensions of this album . . . the band's music has been compared with Led Zeppelin, something that I do not agree with. I would say they were on the same lines as The Who but that's purely on an energy level . . .'

— *Sounds* (on the LP)

'First off, let me admit that Queen are a group whose music I can't really get on with and this album isn't changing my mind. Reputed to have enjoyed some success in the States it's currently in the balance whether they'll really break through here. If they do then I'll have to eat my hat or something . . . Queen are exceptionally derivative of some of the styles of Deep Purple, Jeff Beck, Led Zep and Yes (the last particularly in the vocals). But, consciously or unconsciously, they've taken the ideas away and completely emasculated them . . . maybe Queen try too hard, but their work sounds over-complicated for their musical abilities . . . there's too much of the slack wrist and not enough balls, putting it plainly . . . there's no depth of sound or feeling and it's hard to see any direct merit in it all . . . the vocal lines are Queen's one and only distinctive stamp. A pity really, but I always suspected the group was a cold fish.'

– *Melody Maker* (on the LP)

But, as they have so often been, the music papers were wrong again. And even if they did not like the group's music, audiences did – as the wildly enthusiastic audiences on that first bill-topping tour around the country proved. At Stirling University a riot broke out in the audience when the group would not do more than three encores; a riot that resulted in two members of Queen's road crew being taken to hospital and two other people being stabbed, as a consequence of which the group had to cancel an appearance the following night in Birmingham. They closed the tour with a concert at the London Rainbow that was sold out nearly a week in advance.

Before the tour ended, however, their promotion had pushed the single 'The Seven Seas of Rhye' into the top ten in all the music papers, and *Queen II* was a hit album. What the critics thought no longer mattered a hang. Queen had found a following of their own. And they have kept it ever since.

When most groups have reached a level of that sort rather suddenly, the usual managerial ploy is either to release a devastating follow-up single which guarantees continued TV bookings and press coverage and so hammers home the initial image

– or the group is quickly taken on either a US tour or a quick promotional trip around Europe in the hope of a quick follow-through from the success in Britain.

In Queen's case, it was the latter ploy, although they had already had a promotional film shown on many TV stations in Europe during the previous autumn, and had also made a return trip to Australia to appear at an open air festival in Melbourne. While touring Britain with Mott the Hoople, they had been invited to accompany the same group on a tour of the US starting the following April, just after their own bill-topping tour of Britain had finished. The offer was accepted and off they went – and it was then that Fate intervened in a very strange way.

After only a few dates in the States, Brian May was taken ill – and on examination by doctors it was found that he had hepatitis, which is a disease requiring compulsory quarantine in the States. The tour came to a quick end. May was rushed home to London and into hospital, where he stayed nearly four weeks before going off to convalesce. And so it was that all the group's plans for the summer of 1974 had to be cancelled, and they even had to abandon a second tour of the US which had been set up for the September when May was taken ill again, this time with a duodenal ulcer.

He carried on writing in hospital, and the group continued to record without him – but it meant that just as they had reached a peak in Britain they disappeared for almost six months.

And it may sound an odd thing to say – but it was the best thing that could have happened to them!

Usually, the managerial trick of making a group temporarily unattainable and out-of-reach is planned at a much later stage in their career: in my book on David Bowie in this same series, you may remember reading how this was planned with consummate skill in his case so that he was made to *appear* a 'star' long before he had really made it. In Queen's case, they had made an enormous impact with that single 'Seven Seas of Rhye' (which really was an outstanding single, whatever the

66

critics may say) and they had followed this up with a major tour of their own in which they had been seen performing live by at least 50,000 people, many of whom had subsequently bought their *Queen II* album. And then suddenly through the pure accident of Brian May's two illnesses, they had had those six months to think, to work in the recording studios, to arrange their next British tour, and to plan all their personal promotion.

That it could not have happened at a better moment was proved by the way they suddenly re-emerged in the autumn of 1974 with a second bill-topping tour that was even more successful than the first; a third single 'Killer Queen' which brought them their first number one placing in the music paper charts – and the album *Sheer Heart Attack* which was promptly recognised as a very important album indeed.

It was as though their career had been planned to happen in waves. But it was all due to the accident of May's ill health, and it seems fairly certain to me that even Queen themselves and the people they were associated with managerially were surprised by the speed with which events moved – although hindsight has a trick of smoothing over memories like that!

Their first public appearance after that long summer's absence was on September 5th at a press reception at the Café Royal in London, where Queen were presented with a Silver Disc to mark sales of 250,000 copies of their LP *Queen II* and as a stunt the model Jeanette Charles, who facially resembles Her Majesty Queen Elizabeth, was booked to make the presentation. The group's publicist, Tony Brainsby, even wrote a speech for her to deliver in best regal style:

'Ladies and Gentlemen, it gives me great pleasure to present Queen with this silver disc for 250,000 sales of their LP *Queen II*.
I understand that over the past few months the band has suffered a set-back with Brian May's illnesses. I am so glad to see that he is now fully recovered and back working with the band on their new LP and single.
I unfortunately missed the band's appearance at the Rainbow

earlier this year. However, I look forward to seeing them later this autumn when they begin their tour in November. Thank you.'

It was an old-fashioned, cheeky stunt in the pop tradition, but it got Queen some photo-coverage after being out-of-sight and out-of-mind since the spring – and Brainsby made sure that the message went home by distributing to the assembled audience of writers and free-loaders a press statement of his own, publicising the new single, which read:

'Look at it this way. Just six months ago QUEEN were an unknown, unproven band with just one album, one single and a supporting tour behind them. They stand now with *Queen II* certified silver (*Queen*, too, made the album charts), a massive hit single, an all-conquering tour of Britain already completed and abroad, a sweeping path laid straight to the door of America's rock 'n' roll Hall of Flame. But the past summer has not been without its frustrations. Queen were half-way through their first-ever American concert tour when guitarist Brian May fell ill. The doctors confirmed hepatitis – the musicians' disease? – and Queen were forced to return to London – there to wait while Brian recovered. Soon, with Brian back on his feet, they were able to start work in Wales on their third album. But again Brian fell ill, and this time an emergency operation, followed by a long and thorough convalescence was the only course. Queen were able to do a little work in the studios, but Brian's presence – such an integral part of their total sound – was sorely missed. The frustrations, physical and psychological, might have overwhelmed a lesser band.
But then Queen are much more than an ordinary band. Above all that fate could throw at them, they had their success behind them, and all their hopes for the future to sustain them.
Now, with nothing but their future successes before them on their inevitable path to the very top, Queen have a new

album and a world-wide tour – beginning with their first British appearances since the early New Year – that justifies in every conceivable way the promise of the early summer.

Brian's looking – and playing – better than ever, and it's the soaring biting guitar that drives *Sheer Heart Attack* towards a level of brilliance (sorry, there's no other word for it) that Queen, already out on their own, have achieved before. Brian's guitar, blended with Freddie Mercury's vocals, Deacon John's bass and the driving rhythms of Roger Meddows Taylor and cloaked in the unique blend of studio wizardry and rough, raw aggression that Queen have made something entirely of their own.

The single, from the album, is "Killer Queen"/"Flick Of The Wrist", rush re-released (as a uniquely justified double A-side) on the 11th of October. The tour begins at the Palace Theatre, Manchester, on 30th October, climaxing with a final concert on 19th November at the Rainbow, London. Queen rule – and it's only a matter of months before the whole world knows it.'

Normally, press releases couched in extravagant language of that kind end up in the wast-paper basket – and are quickly forgotten. But, for once, the hard sell was justified. Brainsby was right.

Just as the group's spring push with their single 'The Seven Seas of Rhye', their album *Queen II* and that tour round the provinces had brought them a much wider following than the press realised they had, so they began their autumn campaign with virtually saturation coverage in the teenage magazines like *Melanie*, *Jackie*, *Fabulous*, *Fan* and *Music Star*, with full-page colour portraits in nearly every one. And then produced that single 'Killer Queen', which really was a cracker. Even the music paper critics could see it this time:

'In this week's list of breakers-already-so-soon-my-life is this Mercury penned ditty that should be a huge hit for them. Gentler than "Seven Seas of Rhye", although you can hear similar guitar work at the end. Knockers can start ringing, Queen have come up with a sound that'll prove they aren't any one-hit band. The record, incidentally, is a double A-side, the other song entitled "Flick Of The Wrist".'

– Record Mirror

'A fearless Fred (Mercury) trills off her ["Killer Queen"] insatiable credentials with great poise, heavily phrased but well deployed vocal and guitar noises embellish the rich texture. It's quite obvious that Queen know their way around the studio and as such, this record should be entrenched at number one by the first week in November, or the second week at the latest!'

– New Musical Express

'A double A-side from Queen. "Killer" tries very hard to be sophisticated and intelligent, but merely substitutes a tasteless and not very clever manipulation of standard images for those qualities. By slicking up the production, with all kinds of vocal effects and phrasing, Queen hope you won't notice how dreadful the song actually is. It's almost as dire as "Flick", which has the band attempting to sound vicious and menacing, with another set of frightfully inept lyrics. Listening to this record is like staring into the dark.'

– Melody Maker

'When a band's been off the road and completely out of the picture for a number of months, it's very hard to get back into the thick of things again. That's one reason why this single is so important for Queen. They couldn't have come back in a better way. It's very, very different from "Seven Seas of Rhye" but the Queen sound is very much there. Freddie Mercury comes through as a distinguished rock vocalist and the backing, although complicated at times, is heard loud and clear. "Killer Queen" is a real rocker, building up ferociously, throughout. It opens with a very nifty clicking fingers routine. "Flick Of The Wrist", slightly weaker than "Killer Queen", is another up-tempo number which jogs along beautifully. Yes, folks, Queen are back, and back to stay this time.'

— Disc

And even out in the provinces, the writers of the weekly record columns, which are often somewhat late in recognising talent, were making their predictions:

'Brian May, Queen's guitar lickeur (*sic*) extraordinaire, has recovered and the gang are at their best. Medium-paced rocker that'll hit the top five with ease. Majestic.'

— Bath Evening Chronicle

'By the time you read this, the single "Killer Queen" on the EMI label from Queen, will possibly be occupying a Top Ten position. A great record, and so different from "Seven Seas of Rhye". Queen are certainly a very talented group and this is my fave single of the month. In fact, I'm so keen on it, I'll even go as far as to say it's going to be a future number one.'

— Herts and Cambs Reporter

'Queen look set to top the charts with their single "Killer Queen". If you can imagine a cross between David Bowie and The Sweet, then you know what to expect from Queen.'

— Bradford Telegraph & Argus

'This dynamically explosive, beautifully executed single shows just what an enormous talent this group has. A number one potential.'

— Peterborough Evening Telegraph

The reviews Queen received for their album *Sheer Heart Attack* were just as ecstatic, and it was material from this album that they mainly featured in their elaborately presented stage show, which opened at the Palace Theatre, Manchester, after a week's rehearsals with all the new amplification and lighting equipment that Trident had hired for the tour (the details of which are discussed in Chapters Four and Five). The tour had been due to finish with another concert at the London Rainbow, but all the tickets for it sold out within two days – and so another night there was added to their itinerary.

It was the same story wherever they appeared around Britain, and in reviewing the show the music paper critics did have the grace to admit that the feverish excitement of the audiences, with crowds on their feet, waving, cheering, clapping and stomping, was something that they had not expected to see. Contrary to most expectations, Queen had broken through as a major international act in the face of almost total rejection by the critics.

Wherever they appeared that autumn – in theatres and city halls all over the country – all the tickets for their concerts were sold long before they arrived in town.

'That was the time that *Sheer Heart Attack* really started to shift in large numbers,' said EMI label manager John Bagnall.

And by then music papers like *Disc* and *Record Mirror* were front-paging Queen in full colour; the more serious music papers like *Sounds*, *Melody Maker* and *New Musical Express* were running full-page features; and even the national press had started mentioning the group regularly. And, naturally enough, they were all fascinated by the fact that Brian May had made his own guitar, and that May, Mercury, Taylor and Deacon all had a much more academic background than most rock stars. The same basic facts were repeated over and over again by practically every national paper – but the point got home. Queen were coming to a peak.

As soon as the British tour ended, Queen took the same elaborately staged show – which had been video-taped by Trident when they were appearing at the Rainbow – around Europe with concerts in Sweden, Norway, Finland, Denmark, Germany, Switzerland, France, Belgium and Holland (and how all this was arranged is explained by their then co-manager Dave Thomas in Chapter Five).

At venue after venue, their show opened with the stage in

QUEEN at the time of 'Killer Queen'

Brian May

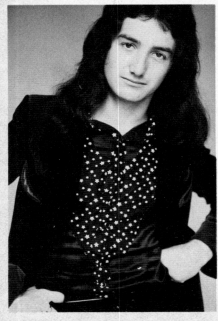

John Deacon

Roger Meddows-Taylor

Fred Mercury

Fred Mercury 1973

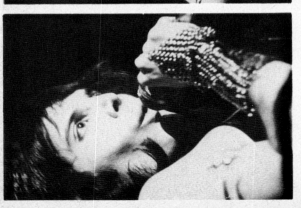

Fred Mercury 1973

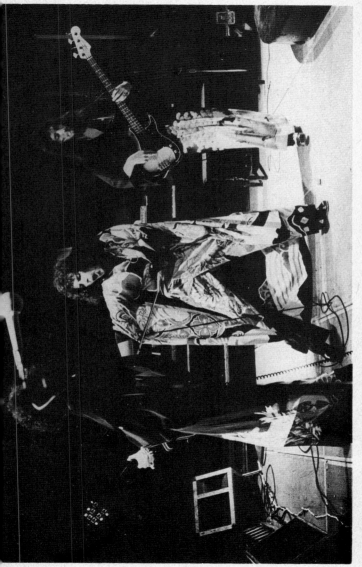

Fred Mercury wearing a kimono he acquired in Japan in April 1975

Brian May holding his handmade guitar

Deacon and Mercury
1972/3

Mercury 1972/3

Mercury in action

Promotional shot at the time of QUEEN II album

QUEEN were presented with their first silver disc by Jeanette Charles in September 1974

At a reception

Japan, April 1975

UEEN

This photograph was originally to promote QUEEN II Album though the same idea was revised for the promotion film for Bohemian Rhapsody total darkness with that one solitary spotlight picking out Freddie Mercury singing 'Now I'm Here' into the microphone, his body erect, his hands clasped, the silver bracelets flopping over his wrists as he reaches for the top notes, and then the burst into the rock section of the song with the lights flashing on and May's guitar, with Deacon's bass and Taylor's drums thundering forth. Everywhere the reaction was the same; it was one of the most exciting stage shows that audiences had ever seen.

There was no doubt about what was happening. The trade paper *Music Week* reported succinctly: QUEEN CONQUER EUROPE.

And so they had, opening in Gothenburg with standing room only – and then going on to Helsinki where every seat had been sold before they left England. There was only one major hitch during the tour. While going under a low bridge, their forty-foot rented articulated lorry which was carrying all the stage lighting and sound equipment got stuck, holding up trains and traffic while furniture vans were quickly hired to empty the lorry and take all the lighting rigs and amplifying equipment on to Munich.

In Hamburg and Munich, manager Dave Thomas said the audiences went wild, and in The Hague in Holland and at Barcelona in Spain, the response was as warm and emotional as that at Manchester at the start of the tour.

After spending Christmas 1974 at home with their families, Queen occupied themselves during January editing down the video-tape of their two Rainbow concerts into a thirty-three minute film, 'Queen At The Rainbow', which has since been circuited in Britain. In January, after John Deacon had married his wife Veronica and the group had released two more tracks from the third album, 'Now I'm Here' and 'Lily Of The Valley' as a fourth single – the band left for the United States, appearing as a bill-topping act in the US for the first time at Columbus, Ohio.

When the first of the annual British music paper polls for 1974/5 was announced, there was no doubt that they really were right up there with The Who, Led Zeppelin and the

Stones: in the *Record Mirror* poll they were voted number two in the British Newcomer section and 'Killer Queen' was voted Second Best Single of the Year; in the *New Musical Express* poll, they were voted Eighth Best British Group, Seventh Best Stage Band, Fourth Most Promising Group in the World section and Third in the British section, and then when the *Disc* poll was announced a few months later they won four sections, Top Live Group, Top International Group, Top British Group and Best Single for 'Killer Queen' while their *Sheer Heart Attack* was voted the number three Best LP of the last year.

It had all happened very suddenly – with the main impetus being that *Sheer Heart Attack* album, the 'Killer Queen' single that they had taken from it, and the strongly visual stage act that the group had carefully constructed around the LP.

Although clearly close to it, they were still not world stars; those concerts they played around the States in February, March and April were the smaller US venues, mostly not holding more than 3,000 to 4,000 fans. They were not yet in the baseball stadium league, although it was now becoming obvious to the hustlers and the wheeler-dealers of the American music business that of all the new bands Queen were most likely to make that next step.

'We later heard that they were being propositioned by would-be managers throughout that tour – without Jack Nelson, who was travelling with them, even being aware that it was going on,' said Dave Thomas, who was co-manager with Nelson.

All this was clearly unsettling the group – but then in mid-April, after a short holiday in the Hawaiian islands, they flew off to Tokyo for the start of a Japanese tour. And it was then that even Queen realised that they really were a world band.

Even before they arrived in Japan, Queen had heard that their earlier albums had been selling well; that they already had their own fan club over there and that 'Killer Queen' was number one in the singles charts. But as the plane landed at

Tokyo Airport and taxied to a standstill, they looked out of the window and saw a crowd of around 3,000 fans waiting for them to step down from the plane.

'They were absolutely amazed – and somewhat overwhelmed,' says Dave Thomas. 'Then, when they went down the steps, there was a large limousine waiting to drive them to their hotel, where there were more crowds of people, milling around in the foyer and in the grounds outside . . . and they discovered to their astonishment that each member of the group had been allocated a bodyguard because it was thought there was a real risk that they might be injured if they left their hotel bedrooms.'

At the Budokan, the Martial Arts Hall in Tokyo, they found that all 10,000 tickets had been sold for their first concert, and that another appearance at the Budokan was being arranged for the last night of their tour – which amounted to more people than they had ever played to before.

Wherever they went in Japan, they were fêted, presented with gifts, treated with deep respect – and Queen loved it. It was the first time they had ever been accepted on this level.

When they returned to London, Freddie told the *Melody Maker*: 'It started the moment we got there, riots at the airport, bodyguards, just like the old Beatle days. The organisation was spellbinding, and we loved every minute of it. Yes, we needed protection. You couldn't go down into the lobby of the hotel, it would be infested, but really nice people, waiting for autographs. And I couldn't believe the crowds at the concerts, all milling about, swaying and singing.'

To *Reveille*, Brian May said: 'They took to us like nothing's ever happened before . . . we're still reeling from it.'

And to *Record Mirror*, Roger Meddows Taylor explained that these 10,000-seater venues had been selling out with the tickets priced at £4.50 to £5.00, and that at one gig there were nearly 500 security staff – and girls had still been carried out unconscious and many more were nearly crushed. 'We hadn't expected anything like it,' he confirmed.

When the tour ended, another large crowd was waiting at Tokyo Airport to see their plane depart – and it was then but

75

one quick journey home and back to their ordinary lives: back to the flat in Holland Park that Freddie had had since his days in Kensington Market; back to the house in Fulham where John Deacon and his wife were making their home; back to the flat in Kew where Roger Meddows Taylor had been living since before Queen's first album was released; back to the anonymity of Kensington where May now had a flat of his own.

The adjustment that had to be made was a great one — because Queen were still just drawing a weekly allowance; they were still living in those homes they had had for three years and more. And the costs incurred in their swift rise to world prominence had been enormous.

It was time to take stock.

CHAPTER FOUR

The key to Queen's success initially was their series of management, publishing and record production contracts with the Trident group of companies – because it was Trident who put up the money that made everything else in their career possible. And that was an enormous sum of money because it was Trident who paid the production costs of their recording sessions, who planned their tours, who paid their publicist, who made all their travel arrangements, who planned their promotion – and paid each member of Queen a weekly sum of money so that they had spending money in their pockets long before their work was bringing in any income.

It is an extraordinary side of Queen's success story and it deserves to be told in full because, so far as I know – and I have interviewed every British artist of any importance over the past fifteen years – this was the first time that an independent record production company had launched a new group of Queen's importance virtually from scratch.

How it all came about was explained to me in a very long and detailed interview with Norman Sheffield, managing director of Centredisc, which is the holding company for the Trident group. It was he who originally founded Trident Studios with his brother Barry, and we discussed how this directly led to the Sheffields' involvement with Queen as we sat talking in Trident's offices in Great Pulteney Street, Soho.

Although Trident had originally been established just as a recording studio, Norman Sheffield said they had received many requests from different artists and managements over the years that they should become more closely involved in record production and even management.

'The first time was in 1968 when I was asked to become involved in joint management of Deep Purple,' said Sheffield. 'I said no and kept on saying no over the years because I realised that a considerable investment would be required, and before going in for that I wanted to wait until Trident was firmly on its feet. Essentially, we were establishing ourselves a firm earning base before going on to invest in any other area of the business,' Sheffield explained.

As Trident became established, it acquired a reputation as a good studio. David Bowie recorded his material there from the time of *Hunky Dory* right through to the *Pin Ups* LP, usually working with Ken Scott. Then Mick Ronson, who played guitar for Bowie, started recording his own solo material at Trident. Harry Nilsson came over from the States and did an album at Trident with Robin Cable, who was to later work on production with Queen. Carly Simon also recorded material at the studios and it was there that Elton John put down the tracks for his earliest albums.

'By 1970 we had reached a stage where we were ready to go on to a further stage in our development as a company,' said Sheffield.

'Many different acts were coming into the studios to record their material, using our engineers. We were coming under pressure from our clients to provide a production service; more and more acts were asking the engineers to act in a production capacity. We discussed this with the engineers and they were keen to move on, too . . . we had a logical situation developing because the studios were so busy that we could now provide our engineers with a career structure. They could come in as first engineers, move on to become second engineers, third engineers and then chief engineers – and it was natural enough that they should want to move on after that. We suggested to our three engineers that they should start producing material themselves and we formed two companies – *Neptune* with Roy Baker and Robin Cable and *Nereus* with Ken Scott.

'We then decided, still in 1970, that the company needed a production A & R Controller (a traditional music business title for an *A*rtists & *R*epertoire executive; someone who guides groups and singers on their choice of material). This was so that we could give a full service more easily. Basically this meant that we needed someone who could be responsible for selecting product.

'At that time we had been working almost solidly for two years with the producer John Anthony, who had been producing material for Rare Bird, Lindisfarne, Genesis and Van der Graaf Generator. He had been hiring a lot of studio time at Trident and we had come to know him well so we brought him in and put him inside Neptune and also at the same time formed Trident Productions.

'The good thing was that we were now in a position to produce different styles of music, which meant that we could spread the work. This progressed along for about six or seven months, and all the boys were having quite a lot of success being asked to produce things. And then the obvious thing happened; people started asking us whether Trident would go into production ourselves.

'By 1971 we had reached the stage where we were prepared to do that. We said OK to the producers and started expanding our sights . . . but there was one thing about which we had to be very careful. It was our golden rule that we would never get involved with an act that was already involved with a record company. This was something that we had to handle very carefully because record companies would often send acts along to us before signing them to a contract, and if we had tried to sign acts in that situation it would have been the death of Trident. No one would have trusted us ever again – so we said we would only go after new unsigned acts.

'John Anthony was looking after all of that side for us, and he brought us three acts in three months. There was Eugene Wallace, an Irish singer that he had found in a folk club, and we made an LP with him. And then there was Mark Ashton, who had been the singer with a group that John had previously produced, Rare Bird, who had had one very big hit, "Sympathy" . . . and there was Queen, whom John had seen one night on one of his wanderings. I think he'd seen them performing in a club.

'Anyway, John came to us and said he had found a band that

79

was worth spending some time on, so my brother Barry went down to see them playing at a hospital dance in Forest Hill and he liked them. By then they were already calling themselves Queen, although they had no management and had cut some rough tracks down at the De Lane Lea studios at their own expense.

'We agreed to sign them along with the other two acts, and our thinking at that stage was that we would record one album with each of the acts and then try to set up a production house deal with one of the major companies for a given number of LPs with a view to Trident having its own label, as and when we were ready. I also went over to the States to have a look at what was happening there to see if we could set up a similar deal for the US.

'By then we had already cut some rough tracks with Queen to see what sort of things were shaping up, and there was considerable discussion over the contractual side. One of the particular things that they were insisting on was that we took on a managerial role as well as a recording and production role. We thought there might be a conflict of interest if we did that, but they were keen that we should. There's no conflict when a band is small, but it tends to grow as it becomes successful and the problems pile up. I'd seen that happen in the past when I'd been associated with another group, Unit 4 Plus 2 – but they were still keen that we should look after management as well.

'In the US I was staying with a friend of mine called Jack Nelson, whom I had known for a couple of years, and I played him the material we'd already recorded with Queen. He was then working with MGM, but I told him that we needed someone at Trident who could take over A & R from an administrative point of view because John Anthony was more interested in recording and finding acts rather than production planning. I suggested to Jack that he might like to come and work in London for a couple of years, which would give John the freedom to do what he liked doing best – and Jack said he would do it. He came over in June 1972, and we finally signed our contracts with Queen on November 1st, 1972.' As he said this Sheffield walked over to a safe, removed a file and showed me the original contracts that Queen had signed.

'For months before they signed we had been paying them wages on an unsigned basis . . . and then when they did sign it was three separate contracts, one management, one publishing, and one recording contract. Later when we came to do our deal with EMI we did a separate deal ourselves with Jack Holzman of Elektra in the States, though unfortunately he left Elektra soon after that. What all this meant was Queen recorded for Trident Audio Productions with EMI releasing their records in the UK and Europe and Elektra issuing their product in the United States, Australia and Japan.

'By the time Queen came to release their first LP, we had made a very heavy investment; we invested several thousand pounds in new equipment; their PA system cost £6,000 and then subsequently we increased that and we bought new instruments for all the members of the band, including a new set of drums – although Brian May had made his own guitar, which was a beautiful instrument. Then their clothes were custom-made at Zandra Rhodes. Our investment started in May 1972, long before they actually signed their contracts. We were purchasing equipment for them, paying them regular weekly wages, and by September of 1972 our investment had reached £15,000,' said Sheffield, who then opened the account books and ledgers for this period to confirm that the group were paid a total of £100 a week at that time.

'That £100 was divided between them so that they each had £25 a week to live on, and then later we doubled that,' he said.

'By the time their first LP was released in July 1973, our total investment had reached £33,000 . . . and by then we had formed the Fan Club for them, and we were bearing expenses like printing biographies and photographs, and arranging their launching party.

'They weren't having to go out on the road because that wasn't the way that we wanted to launch them; throughout this period they only did about a dozen gigs, which were mainly ballrooms and colleges so that they could get used to working together in front of an audience again. We launched the band publicly again at the Marquee, although by the time the first album was released it had been lying on the shelf for months. I think we actually completed that first LP in 1972, and then it took nearly a year to set up the deal with the record company.

'By then Trident had been advancing them for a year, paying them their money and buying all their equipment – and all that was before we even recouped one penny from EMI, who only paid us a very small advance for that first album. On the first Queen LP we had an advance from EMI of £4,000, and then on *Queen II* we had an advance of £7,000, which didn't even begin to cover the costs of production. We also issued a single to coincide with the first LP and made a promotional film at Trident's expense which was shown on "The Old Grey Whistle Test" and in a number of overseas territories. But this was something we could do because we had a film production company within the Trident set-up; we had all the tools in the house. Our main idea in making that film was that we thought we'd be able to take it round the business creating interest in the group.

'One man we showed the film to was Bob Hirschmann, an old friend of ours who was managing Mott the Hoople, and he agreed and Mott agreed that Queen could be the support act when Mott made a British tour in the autumn of 1973, although that had to be subsidised by us.

'For that tour with Mott the Hoople, Trident hired the lighting and also extra supporting PA equipment, and prior to that tour, by September 1973, our total investment in Queen had reached £62,976.26,' said Sheffield, reading out the pounds and the pence from his ledgers, showing how the sums paid had reached this total in what was always called the 'Queen Advance Account'. 'The books have been audited twice since then,' he said as he confirmed that extraordinary figure of £62,976.26.

When I commented that I was unaware of any other British group being launched on such a budget, he said: 'Thank you – I don't think people do realise how much Trident put into the group. But I think you'd have to make an investment of those dimensions today because the music business has grown into such a vast industry with all the costs escalating accordingly.'

Of that first tour with Mott the Hoople, when Queen received ovations at concert after concert, Sheffield said: 'The tour was a success artistically, although not commercially – but we expected that. And it was that tour that gave us the opportunity of Queen going to tour the States with Mott, which they did after making their first solo tour of Britain – that was the American tour that was cut short because of Brian May's illness. As soon as it was confirmed that he had hepatitis, we had to rush him home very fast indeed because that's a quarantine disease in the States. We were able to arrange it quickly because one of our directors had a brother who was a surgeon at Bart's, and through him we were able to get Brian into Guy's Hospital and into private care, where he stayed for three or four weeks. When he came out we sent him on holiday to recuperate while the boys carried on working on the *Sheer Heart Attack* LP without him, doing as much work as they could, leaving the guitar parts to be added when he came back.

'Their solo tour was planned for November, opening at the Manchester Palace – and we'd lost so much time that we only just managed to complete the album in time. By then we were starting to get sales for their records, but it was *Sheer Heart Attack* that did the volume. And it was only then that we started getting money back in the form of recoupment. But also by then we were already writing the budget for *Sheer Heart Attack*, and that cost £28,000. Just as we were about to begin that tour, Freddie went sick for one day – and you can imagine the panic that caused. But he recovered very quickly.

'By then they had reached the stage where management matters were taking up more and more time, and Dave Thomas was now sharing the management with Jack Nelson. The group still didn't think there was any conflict of interest between us, possibly because we were still laying out the cash, but I'd always thought there was a risk in a situation like that – which was why when they did sign their contracts with us I'd made the management contract a shorter one than those for publishing and recording.'

(There is a gap in the narrative with Norman Sheffield here because Dave Thomas told me the story of how the Mott tour was arranged, what happened following *Sheer Heart Attack* and his story is told in the next chapter.)

Sheffield went on to tell me quite candidly that the situation which had developed, with nearly all Queen's financial and other business affairs being handled from within the Trident office, was one in which a conflict of interest could very easily have arisen at any time. He was very open about this, and said with a conviction possibly enhanced by hindsight, that it was unfortunate that Queen did not have a separate management right from the start.

'I think any group needs to have someone to represent them in their dealings with their record company and their producers, and that's the role that a manager would fulfil, among a great many other things,' he said.

'When the row eventually erupted between the group and ourselves, they said that our interests were too close, although I must say that unlike some people in this business we *never* deducted management commission from record royalties. In the business it has been known for both record production *and* management commissions to be deducted from royalties, but we never did that.

'I think the problems between us and the group really started when they were over in the States in 1975 on their second US tour. They were travelling with Jack but no matter how well a group is looked after there is always a lot of stress and pressure during those long American tours. They were beginning to feel their feet at that time as a band, and yet at the same time they were creating larger and larger debts. You can't have your cake and eat it in this business any more than you can in any other, but I think there was some non-comprehension of the financial implications of some of the things we'd done – even though we'd always done them with the group's knowledge. We also got the impression that Freddie and Jack weren't getting on too well in the States, and then Jack and I broke our relationship up and he went back to America. We sat down and discussed everything with the band both prior to Jack going and immediately afterwards, and they seemed to be quite happy. We explained that Dave would be handling the front-line situation with me handling the back-line situation, and they seemed to go along with that . . . and then about two weeks after that conversation we had fairly hefty demands from the band for fairly large sums of money.

'We got together with them to discuss the matter, and they were advised by me and by their own accountants that it would be wrong to ask for the money, and, indeed, wrong to accept it from a financial point of view because of the tax implications . . . but it was after that that we said perhaps we should all agree to sever the management relationship. By then they already had their own accountant and their own lawyer working for them, and on a personal level I knew that I could not get through to them.

'By that time our investment in the band was running around the £190,000 level. We had in the pipeline sums of money coming back to them and to us which cancelled some of that out, but £190,000 was the total debt, and as far as we were concerned we had not agreed to cross-collateralise (the particular technicality of the situation was that they were due considerable sums in record royalties and there was no legal obligation on them to pay us). It was around this time that we discussed that while they were touring in the States they were already being approached by other managers offering them deals without Jack even knowing that they'd been discussing the matter. And, of course, in a situation like this these other people had been saying: "You should have that money, Freddie!" And there was no way that Freddie was going to turn round and say, "But I owe Trident £190,000!" Of course, groups do get propositions of different kinds when they start touring the States; people approach the business so differently over there. So much hustling goes on, but I think all this was complicated by the fact that the group themselves were beginning to realise what a hot property they had become. Basically, our dispute with them was over money,' said Sheffield.

One of the aspects of my conversation with Norman Sheffield that impressed me was that at no time did he say anything that was in any way uncomplimentary about the group – and he went out of his way to stress the fact that the manager they eventually signed with, John Reid, was not one of those people that had been badgering them in the States. Indeed, I later heard from another source that it was Queen themselves who approached Reid through an intermediary *after* their dispute had developed with Trident.

'We were happy to agree that they should resolve the management situation, and we agreed to bring forward the date on which our own management contract would expire,' said Sheffield. 'But we did ask if we could see the short-list they were drawing up as we had a right of assignment under our contract. They came to us and told us of the various offers they had received, some of them from very good managers. And when they decided on John Reid, we were pleased for them – they could not have found a better bloke!

'Right up to that point we were thinking that they would appoint their own management and that we would continue to look after the record production and publishing side, but then they said: "We would rather go the whole way." We thought it was madness for them to want to leave us at that time when they were so much in debt to Trident, but that was what they wanted to do. We pointed out to them that if they left us under such a situation, they would be creating even more debt. But they were determined to leave – and so we agreed on a severance of contract and we also allowed the band to slow down to one LP a year. Had we been a bull-nosed record company, we could have said "Fuck it!" And we could have demanded that they give us the two LPs a year that were in the contract.

'In addition, it was agreed that a sum of money be paid to us on severance of the contracts and that we should retain a percentage of their earnings on albums that we have not been able to complete under our contracts with them. We have also retained our rights to all the old product and the film that was made of them at the Rainbow in any combination. We can release compilation LPs and we have also got a live *Queen At The Rainbow* LP that has never been released. And having agreed all that we agreed to sever the contracts. We could have done it another way: we could have put everything on suspension and frozen everything – but that's a terrible thing to do to an artist. I think the way it was resolved was the best way out of the situation because it means that all the money that we spent will be recouped and we left the new management in a situation where a new LP was being recorded, and the LP was ready to roll, all the investment having been made – all John Reid really had to do was pull the right buttons and he'd got it. And we even gave them an extended period of time to pay us the severance payments. Our publishing contract has lapsed with this last album, but we do have a percentage of their next six albums.

'I would not like it to be thought that we have been totally philanthropic,' said Sheffield. 'We haven't. We have been tough. But we have been totally fair. I don't think it's trumpet-blowing but we think we let them go as gentlemen. There are many other people in our position who had they had the contracts that we had would have put the group under suspension and forced them to pay £1,000,000. The one thing that we recognised throughout this very difficult situation was that we stood the chance of smashing the band if we didn't handle it all carefully. They are a naturally highly strung band, who are tense and live on their nerves, and we had to think of all that.

'But looking back on it all now, I can see the problem – to make a band happen that quickly you need to have all the control, but the very fact of having all that control is a built-in trap. There are going to be demands from the band in which a manager would say yes and their record company would say no. Nowadays any major band is in the situation where vast investments are required, and where initially you may lose money rapidly. For a US tour you can easily work to a budget of £60,000, expecting only to make £2,000 at the end of it, and that leaves very little margin if someone falls ill in the middle of the tour and dates have to be cancelled.

'So far as Queen were concerned, we saw this budgetary problem when they were recording. They would start on an album with a budget of £10,000 – and then when it was running at £25,000 we would agree with their artistic feelings and let them go along with it.

'They would like to think they are good businessmen. They certainly take an interest in all the right things, although if Freddie was a bank manager he wouldn't be as good as a singer! I can't sing like Freddie and although I've been playing drums longer than Roger Taylor, he is ten times better than I am.

'We were no angels. We made mistakes. I don't think it happened too fast. If Trident made a mistake then the mistake was mine – and possibly I did not learn soon enough that Jack Nelson's dealings were far more biased towards an artistic relationship than a business relationship. When David joined the company he came in as an anchor man, but by then it was too late, by then they wanted to live on the level of the artists they were, and although their records were starting to sell well in the States all the money was eighteen months down the line. You can fix up bridging finance in a situation like that – but it's not the moment to have a new light rig costing £25,000!

'And then I think there was another, more personal problem, too, which a great many artists feel at one stage in their career: they travel the world, staying in the best hotels, flying by plane, and being treated royally wherever they go and then at the end of it all they come back to London and their little flats in Notting Hill Gate. And there's a terrible de-gearing process because it all changes so suddenly like going away on a beautiful dream holiday-of-a-lifetime, coming back on Sunday – and starting work on Monday morning. I think there was a bit of that after they had so much success in Japan – and then had to come straight back to London.

'They trusted us for long enough, but then it got to the point where they were not sure . . . and the time of strength came when they said, "We will not do this unless we get some cash." The relationship that we had with them was like a love affair in a way – with all the heights and depths of that situation. On both sides. And then at the end of the affair the only solution was to get a divorce.'

Finally, I asked Norman Sheffield how he saw the group now.

Of Freddie Mercury, he said: 'There is no question that Freddie Mercury couldn't have become a star – but he might have taken a different route had he not worked with us. He could have been destroyed had he been with a hard management. He is volatile, very talented, charming . . . he is concise, but often confused. He is positive in his direction, but not always sure how to get there.'

Of Brian May, he said: 'He is the out-and-out thoroughbred musician. He is totally introvert, but a musician through and through.'

Of Roger Taylor, he said: 'He always wanted to be a drummer in a rock 'n' roll band, but there are latent twinges of him going in other directions later on; I think he'll want to get other things in life.'

Of John Deacon, he said: 'He's the deep one. He tends to be good for the others as a stabilising influence. He acts more maturely than the others possibly because his musical involvement is not as deep as the other three . . . he tends to be the spokesman for the band in private, although he is the least receptive in public. In private he is only half the musician; in public, the musician comes to the forefront.'

CHAPTER FIVE

Dave Thomas first saw Queen at the Pheasantry in the Kings Road, Chelsea, when the group was performing before an invited audience of executives from different record companies. It was at the time that Trident were trying to set up a package deal for Queen, Eugene Wallace and Mark Ashton with one of the major companies on a licensing basis, hoping that they might also be given their own label.

'This night at the Pheasantry was intended to be a showcase for them, but they bombed out completely,' said Thomas, whom I interviewed separately at the Trident offices on three different occasions. It was he who was brought in by Norman Sheffield to be the co-manager for Queen when the group's career started to develop.

'That show at the Pheasantry just went wrong. We'd invited all these different people along hoping that there'd be widespread interest in Queen, but the whole thing just didn't work,' he said. 'The noise was too much, and after that they were turned down by several companies . . . and then around the time of the Midem Festival in 1973 we'd got a couple of companies interested again and Roy Featherstone of EMI, to whom we played the tapes out in Midem, asked us not to sign anything with anyone until he got back. At the same time we were still looking for management for Queen, but no one wanted to know – and in the end we decided to manage them ourselves.'

Thomas said the actual production costs of that first album, which Queen had completed long before the deal was done with EMI, totalled £13,000, and then the second LP cost a further £20,000.

'What cost all the money was the intricacy of their work,' he said. 'Everything had to be done just right. That was a fetish with the group and they'd spend days in the studio working on overdubs and vocal harmonies . . . the main underlying reason for it costing so much was that they had this drive for perfection. They would not accept anything unless the sound was spot on. Brian and Fred were the two perfectionists in the band, searching for the perfect tonal quality for each song, studying the phasing of the stereo mix. There was always just the four of them in the studio, and then if anything went wrong arguments would break out – if an outsider walked in he would think they were ripping each other to pieces. And then after a row like that they wouldn't talk to each other for a day or so. The rows were usually over the material or the arrangements.

'From the beginning the tonal quality of Brian's guitar pieces was something that they were always trying to perfect, because they realised that this was one of the highlights of their recorded sound . . . they were always a high tension band, living off their nerves. That was what they were like when they first started recording, and they haven't changed; they'll always be like that, and it's been an important ingredient in their success.

'Sometimes late at night plates and glasses that had been brought in with their food and drink would go flying across the studio. Why? Release – just release. As I said before, there was always so much tension. They were a nervous band.

'This was something that was usually seen only in the studio, but I remember once when it became very visible on stage. That was when they visited Leeds University during their second bill-topping tour in November 1974. There was one particular monitor system that wasn't working on stage – Roger's – and because of this he could not hear himself properly, and so the only way he could increase the level of his monitor system was to indicate that he wanted to do this to his monitor mixer, and still it didn't happen. Consequently after he had walked off stage he tried to kick down the panel in his dressing room, and then had to be whisked away to Leeds Infirmary in his stage clothes because he had severely bruised his foot.

'And during a concert in another tour Roger was so upset because of the stage sound, and so was Brian during that concert, that he walked out and completely destroyed his drum kit at the end of the set. In *his* anger Brian had thrown his guitar across the stage and had bent half the tuning frets. There was always tension when they were working, like a flash-point situation, and then minutes later after they'd got back to their dressing room they would be very concerned about what had happened to their equipment on stage. Roger would always be anxious that his drum kit would be all right next day.

'After a show was over, they'd start to wind down. They were always party-goers, although never heavy drinkers; they'd unwind by going out in a party for a meal or by sitting around in hotel rooms meeting people . . . and then next day they wouldn't get up until around twelve o'clock when they'd have some breakfast and their vitamin pills before going on to the next gig. The vitamin pills were almost a ritual like taking salt tablets after they'd lost a lot of salt during a concert. They'd take about twelve vitamin pills a day, as well as being a high tension band they are not beefy people; they are light in stature, eating up their energy all the time living on their nerves . . . and they have to have all those vitamin pills because when you're on tour you get very stodgy meals and often don't eat regularly; the vitamins are just a replacement.

'The start of everything for them, really, was that Mott the Hoople tour. Before that they'd made hardly any live appearances, at the most a dozen gigs, but maybe not much more than four. This was intentional because it was the policy of Trident that the band would never be seen out working anywhere other than under the right conditions – the right lighting, the right sound system, and so on. We didn't want to dilute the effect we hoped they were going to create by them being seen in all the pubs and clubs . . . they never went through a period of going out on gigs at £20.00 a night because we didn't try to set them up. When they did start that tour with Mott the Hoople, they had John Harris to be their sound mixer. He had been a friend of theirs right from the beginning, and we brought in James Dann to look after the light show, having heard of him by word of mouth.

'Our idea right from the start was that Queen would come

into the business at the right level; that was a definite policy of the company – and for six or nine months beforehand they were all, John Harris included, on a weekly retainer so that they didn't have to do anything else. It all started to take shape, really, around the time of the third album, *Sheer Heart Attack*. That was when their records started to sell, and their stage show developed.

'They had spent a long time working on that album, routining all the songs down at Rockfield studios and then coming back to London to put down the basic backing tracks before coming back to Trident to do the overdubs and the re-mixing. They had really worked at this, seven days a week, twenty-four hours a day because they'd got a deadline to work to and time to make up after Brian's illness. All told that album took three months to produce and the costs came to around £28,000 to £30,000. It was more complex than anything they had done before, which was why the costs kept growing like that, but when it was released it was acclaimed as an excellently produced LP.

'When they finally finished *Sheer Heart Attack*, there was only a few days to go before the tour was due to start so then they had to go straight into detailed planning of their stage act. That was done down at Liveware Studios in Ealing, where they rehearsed the different numbers and tried out the equipment . . . and it was only then, I think, that it began to dawn on everyone just what size of show we were taking out. Just to carry all the equipment we had to have a forty-foot articulated lorry *and* a ten ton truck. On top of that we had a road crew of fifteen plus a chauffeur-driven limousine for them. We just had the one week's rehearsal and then we all moved off to Manchester, where the show was due to open.

'It was costing a fortune, hiring all their equipment. There was their sound equipment, the light show and all their own backline equipment, and all of this had to be rigged and de-rigged every day.

'This meant that at every venue the road crew had to be there by ten am each day to start setting up the equipment since the set-up time was about six hours, and then at four pm every day

93

there would be the sound-check. That was when the group arrived, and then they would take two to two and a half hours to complete each sound check much to the annoyance of the support band . . . and then some days they would just be left with enough time for a bath and a meal before they'd have to go on and do their set. At eleven pm after they had finished their set, the road crew would start dismantling all the equipment – and this de-rigging process would take another three hours every night.

'Often this would mean that at around three am in the morning the road crew would start driving off to the next town – while the band were just getting to sleep after the show. And then come ten am the next day the whole thing would start all over again, with the road crew catching up on their sleep during the day after they'd set up the equipment. I think that was the first time that a tour had been planned on such a scale and with so much equipment in this country, although that's often the way it's done in the States.

'Anyway, the first gig was at Manchester Palace – and it was immediately successful. Everything they'd got had been thrown into this tour and the audience could see it. The excitement was intense. About eighty per cent of the audience just leapt out of their seats and rushed the stage, and for the first time we had great difficulty getting the group off the stage without being ripped to pieces; there was also an enormous crush outside the stage door, something that they hadn't experienced before.

'By the next night, when they were appearing at Hanley, we had tightened up on the timing so that there was no risk of them being hurt as they left the stage. We had the limousine standing right outside the stage door, and then as they left the stage they could run through the back of the house, out through the door and into the limousine, and be away within sixty seconds of the performance finishing – and within four minutes of leaving the stage they were back at their hotel. That was how we stopped them being mobbed.

'Sometimes there would be a problem if the entrance to the

stage door was narrow and we couldn't back the limousine up to the door – then we would have half the road crew standing round the stage door to shield the group as they left the theatre, but this was never easy because the Queenies were always very good with their fans. They would always insist on stopping to sign autographs so what we'd try to do was get them into the limousine so that the programmes or photographs that the fans wanted signed could be passed in through the window without the group being in any danger of getting hurt.

'Another thing that worried us right at the beginning was that Fred had this habit of going right to the front of the stage so that he came very close to touching the fans. Brian would sometimes do this, too, and the road crew and the bouncers would be worried in case something happened. At Glasgow Apollo, it did. As Fred came to the front, a guy in the audience grabbed hold of Fred's microphone lead and pulled him into the audience – and the bouncers and road crew had to go diving in to rescue him – he never tried that trick again after that.

'The other thing that started happening on that tour was that fans began throwing presents on to the stage – rings, bracelets, cushions, dolls, all sorts of things. Brian had said in one interview that he liked penguins, and all sorts of gifts with a penguin motif started landing on the stage, and there were pillowcases with the "Queen" motif beautifully embroidered, things that the fans must have spent hours working on.

'The noisiest reception came at the Glasgow Apollo, where there was more damage done that night than at any other pop concert in three or four years. The first ten rows of seats were broken, and yet strangely although this violence broke out the band themselves are very gentle people, and their music is adult music – in no way could they be compared with the Bay City Rollers or David Essex. Yet that night there was the sort of pandemonium you normally only get at a teenybop concert. The group themselves are always happiest when they get a listening-audience; that's when *they* get excited.

'On that tour in the autumn of 1974 we ended up at the

Rainbow, which they regarded as a very important gig because they themselves lived in London. To them, the Rainbow was the big testing ground – and they were a little apprehensive about this because London audiences do have a reputation for being very much cooler than the rest of the country; but at the Rainbow exactly the same thing happened as had happened throughout the tour. They had a reception afterwards at the Swiss Cottage Holiday Inn, and everyone there was over the moon with excitement . . . they'd had the kind of response from the audience that they'd been dreaming of – and people had been screaming for particular numbers like "Liar", "Keep Yourself Alive" and "Stone Cold Crazy".

'After the concert all the equipment had to be packed up and taken over to Scandinavia at the start of their fifteen-day tour of Europe, which took them to Gothenburg, Helsinki, Oslo, Munich, Cologne, Hamburg and then on to Barcelona – and the same thing happened throughout the European tour that had already been happening in Britain. The audiences went wild, although the thing that surprised me was the feeling of shock that one could sense in the audience who didn't seem used to seeing a live show presented with that amount of stage equipment. As the show started, the people in the auditorium were just sitting there with their mouths open, until in the second half the usual pandemonium broke out. In Spain, the group were relatively unknown but in Barcelona all 6,000 tickets for their concert were sold and for the group themselves I felt that musically that was one of the most amazing concerts they had ever done. It all went right that night.'

Since that tour cinema audiences in other parts of the country have been able to see just how far Queen had advanced by the autumn of 1974. Both their concerts at the Rainbow were video-taped, and then the group themselves spent nearly four weeks on the post-production process, editing the sequences down into the thirty-three-minute film 'Queen At The Rainbow', which was the supporting movie to the Burt Reynolds–Catherine Deneuve film 'Hustle' in the spring of 1976.

Norman Sheffield was the film's executive producer with

Bruce Gowers as its director and James Dann responsible for the lighting. It is worth seeing if you get the chance because it shows how Queen's music was developing, although it is noticeably more raw than the sound they were to produce a year later at the time of the release of the LP *A Night At The Opera*.

Some of their stage numbers are not included in the film, but, as on the tour, it opens after a few preliminary shots of them arriving at the theatre in their limousine and preparing for the concert backstage, with the theatre shrouded in darkness and that solitary spotlight picking out the swirling costume of Freddie Mercury for the opening number, 'Now I'm Here'. It is on the next number, 'So Sad', that one realises what a gentle drummer Roger Taylor can be with the cymbals rustling like waves in the background accompanying the soaring pure notes of May's guitar. Other numbers that are featured are 'Killer Queen', with Mercury playing piano; 'March Of The Black Queen', 'Keep Yourself Alive', their show-stopping 'Liar', 'Stone Cold Crazy' and the finale 'Lap Of The Gods'.

Throughout the time that they were working on the *Sheer Heart Attack* album, planning the stage act and then touring Britain and Europe, Queen were constantly afraid that illness would undermine all their efforts again, just as it had brought their first US tour with Mott the Hoople to a premature end when Brian May collapsed with hepatitis.

'After that experience, the band always had this fear that just when they were ready for another major step forward illness would intervene,' said Dave Thomas. 'They were always nervous about this, and being on the road was always a problem because of the hardships of long hours, not enough sleep and irregular meals. After that first US tour there was always this constant fear that something might happen again. I mention this because during the British and European tours it became noticeable towards the end that Freddie had started coughing a lot, although after they'd rested over the Christmas period he settled down again.

'There'd been some talk about this cough, but we thought he'd got over it, and at the end of January they left for the

States and the start of their second tour of North America, still basically using the same stage act that they'd now been working on for some months. They'd been hoping originally to go back to the States the previous September but that had had to be cancelled because of Brian May's second illness, so you can imagine how anxious they were that nothing should go wrong this time.

'The tour started off well. It was the first time they'd head-lined in the States, and the demand for tickets was so great that they started doubling up on shows, instead of just doing the one show a night in each venue at around eight pm, they started doing a six pm and an eight thirty pm concert each night in Boston and New York, and the concerts were still completely sold out.'

The tour started off in Columbus, Ohio, on February 5, and then they moved on to Cincinatti (6th), Dayton (7th), Cleve-land (8th), South Bend (9th), Detroit (10th), Toledo (11th), had a short break and began again at Waterbury (14th), Boston (15th), New York (16th), Trenton (17th), Lewiston, Maine (19th), Passaic (21st), Harrisburg (22nd) and then Philadelphia (23rd).

'By the time we got to Philadelphia, the strain was begin-ning to show in Freddie's voice. He'd always been one for liv-ing it up after gigs, something you expect because there's enormous excitement in the air after playing a concert . . . but now he'd started going to bed early to rest his voice because he was finding that he could not hit the high notes properly, and was having to drop his voice, and this had been gradually getting worse until Philadelphia, where we had two shows arranged, and on the morning afterwards Fred could hardly speak; and this was aggravated by the dry central heating that they'd had to live with in all the hotels, which was also affect-ing his throat.

'On the next morning after Queen's appearance at the Erlinger Theatre in Philadelphia, Fred's throat was so bad that we took him round to the Philadelphia University Hospital to see a throat specialist, who examined him and gave as his analysis that Fred had two nodes through having over-strained his voice. In the doctor's opinion, Fred should take three months' complete rest – well, you can imagine the depression that caused.

'We couldn't break the news to the others because they'd gone on ahead to Washington, where the group was due to appear that night at the John F. Kennedy Center. Jack Nelson and I had stayed behind in Philadelphia with Fred to see what happened at the hospital. When he was told that there would be no more gigs for another three months, he was in a state of utter depression. He felt that he had let the fans down and the rest of the band down. "The band will kill me," he said.

'On their first visit to the States with Mott, everything had gone wrong as well – and now Fred felt that he was to blame, and he felt it acutely because ever since that Mott tour he had always said rather gloomily whenever future plans were discussed that they'd all come to nothing because someone would go ill again.

'Anyway, we were now well into the day – and Fred was quite determined to go ahead with that night's show in Washington because the tickets had all been sold, and by then the rest of the group would be waiting at the John F. Kennedy Center for him to arrive. We went to the station in Philadelphia to catch a train to Washington, and after we'd bought the tickets and gone through into the station hall and caught the train we settled down for the journey to Washington, discussing what we'd do with the concerts that were scheduled throughout March. Then just outside Baltimore the train came to a halt, and we all had to get off because there had been a derailment. We found ourselves stuck in Baltimore in a little station bar, and because of this derailment all the rent-a-cars had been hired, all the taxis had been booked, and the airport was closed because of fog . . . it was now coming on for five o'clock, and Fred was due on stage with the group at eight pm that night in Washington. You can imagine the tension that was developing because there was no way that we could communicate with the group to let them know where we were and what was happening.

'We tried every possible means of getting to Washington – bus, hired car, taxi, private plane. And everything had gone. And then just as we were all on the point of despair an announcement came over the station loud speaker system that one train was coming through direct to Washington – but it had no spare seats. So we booked two whole compartments of sleepers, and then lay down on the bunks on this endlessly slow train, waiting for it to arrive in Washington.

'By the time we got to the JFK Center, we had missed the sound check, and we still hadn't been able to contact the other members of the group who had all been there at the Center waiting for us to arrive. We eventually got to Washington at seven-fifteen pm with the group due to go on stage at eight, which gave us just enough time to get to the hotel where the others were staying. We broke the news to them that Fred had been advised not to sing for another three months, and they accepted it very well, although obviously they were most upset about the whole thing. And then they got in the car for the drive to the Kennedy Center for what they now thought would be the last concert of their tour, and they went on stage and did the most amazing gig that I have ever seen them do in my life. It was an amazing show because they seemed to have so much energy, and to our astonishment there was Freddie hitting all the high notes again.

'After that we thought we should take another opinion on his throat, and we went to see another doctor, this time in Washington, having by then pulled out of five concerts – and he gave us the opinion that they were not nodes at all, but simply swellings in the throat. And this second doctor said that in his view Freddie would need to give his voice some rest, but that there would be no need for him to have an operation, which was what the first doctor had told us.

'After getting that second opinion, which was so different to the first, we decided to get a third to make sure, and this time we went to the top show business throat specialist in New York who advises Tom Jones, Barbra Streisand, and people like that, and he confirmed that it was just a swelling and that what Freddie should do was rest his voice as much as he could, avoid talking to people, and take some anti-biotics; so having received that news, we decided to confirm the cancellation of concerts in Pittsburgh, Kutzton, Buffalo, Toronto, London and Davenport and then resume the tour again at La Crosse, cancelling further concerts at intervals during the tour so that Fred didn't have to overwork his voice.

'The whole schedule for that tour was de-geared, and whereas we had been planning to appear in forty-eight concerts, the group ending up playing thirty-three . . . but we still had all the lighting equipment and the sound system to pay for and so instead of making a small profit on that tour, we came out of it with a loss. We were in a position where we had the same outgoings that we had planned for in the first place, but an income from ticket sales that was far short of what we had been budgeting for.

'After playing the last concert in Seattle, the group went off to a small island, Kavai, in the Hawaiian islands so that they could rest and relax while all their equipment was air-freighted on to Tokyo, where they were due to begin a Japanese tour at the Budokan hall on April 19th. It was Jack's idea that they should go to Kavai; he thought they needed somewhere quiet with few other holidaymakers around after all the excitement of the US tour.

'And they did rest in Kavai before flying on to Tokyo, where they arrived a couple of days before their first gig, where their career really moved on into a different phase. To their astonishment, there were thousands of fans waiting for them at the airport. It was the first time they had ever had a reception like this, although they had heard in advance that their albums had been selling well in Japan.

'I think they all found it quite overwhelming, seeing so many young fans crowding the airport, shouting, screaming and waving just for them, and then being whisked away through the crowd in their limousine to their hotel, where they found another crowd waiting outside . . . it was the first time that they had ever had to have bodyguards, and the first time they had had to stay confined to their hotels because of the vast numbers of people standing in the street trying to see them. There'd been one small clue that something unusual was happening out in Japan in that the amount of fanmail we were receiving from there was quite disproportionate to that coming in from the rest of the world, but until the group actually stepped off the plane they had no idea just how popular they were in that country.

'Every day piles of presents from fans were taken to their hotel, beautiful drawn pictures, paintings and caricatures; specially dressed dolls, ornate fans, pieces of silk, all of them very fine quality.

'Because of the fan mail, we had had this feeling that their music would go down well in Japan – but none of us were expecting this. The promoters told us that all 10,000 tickets had been sold for their appearance at the Budokan, the Martial Arts Hall, so then they agreed to do another concert and that sold out, too, which was quite incredible. As each day developed, I think they became more and more surprised by the strength of the reaction – it was because of it that the Japanese promoters, Watanabe, had provided Freddie, Brian, Roger and John each with his own bodyguard (Fred's was a karate and judo expert who only stood about four foot two inches tall!) But the trouble was that even though they had this protection, they dare not leave their hotel without the most careful organisation.

'On one of their days off, they spent the day at the home of the promoter, who had a typically Japanese house, built in the traditional style, which they all found very interesting; then another time there was a reception at which they met the British Ambassador to Japan. I think what so excited them was that they all, particularly Fred, had this idealised view of what Japan would be like. He had always said in interviews that this was the one place he was anxious to go to, and then when they actually arrived there to be treated so well, and looked after with the utmost courtesy by their hosts, confirmed all their preconceived ideas. They just fell in love with the place and with the people, and in turn they were treated like kings. It was the first time this had ever happened to them in this way, and they knew that it was their music that had done it for them.

'For the first of their shows at the Budokan, they presented precisely the same stage show that had originally been staged at the Palace Theatre in Manchester the previous autumn. It was the largest audience they had ever played to as a headline act and so this made the reaction for the group even more dramatic. Fred had taken the trouble to learn a little Japanese, and when he went to the microphone and said "It's nice to be here in Tokyo" – that went down very well. At the end of that first gig the crowd around the theatre was so intense that they had to be driven in an armoured truck, which again was a totally new experience for them.

'Before their last concert in Tokyo, they all went out and bought traditional Japanese kimonos and after doing their act when they went back on stage to do an encore they did so wearing the kimonos, and the audience just went wild because it was a visual way of the Queenies themselves saying "thank you".

'Fred brought back presents from Japan for all the girls in the Trident office, kimonos and other silks for his girlfriend Mary Austin, and heaps of dolls and other gifts, including a very old samurai sword for himself with which he was delighted. They all had so many gifts given to them out there that they each had a huge packing case stacked with nothing but presents, and when they arrived back at Heathrow Airport it took them an hour and a half to pass through Customs.

'Everything about the trip had been a revelation to them; to have that crowd of people outside their hotel was exciting enough but when they travelled by train to give concerts in other cities in Japan, the fans had somehow discovered the time

103

and the route that they were taking and there were crowds waiting to see them on the platform of every station their train passed through, which was quite amazing. Then travelling between the cities they found the beauty of the countryside quite stunning. There was something, too, in the way that the audiences related to Freddie; his face is slightly oriental in appearance and in some strange sort of way this and the combination in music of the intricacy of their songwriting and then the occasional violence of their music seemed to touch off something in the audiences. It was as though their music was directly relating to the Japanese themselves, who are very delicate people in many ways and yet who can be very violent; it was as though some sort of chemical relationship had been established between Freddie and the audience.

'At the end of the tour, they went to the airport in Tokyo to catch their plane back to England, and there was another crowd waiting to wave goodbye. I think the contrast in being treated like that and then flying straight back to London and back to their flats must have been an enormous thing for them to have to adjust to. It was back to "good old England", and their old humdrum way of life. The contrast was even more acute because when they had left in February "Killer Queen" had been their most successful record and they had also had a great success with the album *Sheer Heart Attack*, and by May it was largely forgotten ... so they had to make this strange adjustment of being at their very peak in Tokyo one day and then flying back to Britain and being just another group the next. I think that was a very difficult time for them.

'When they returned, they took about four weeks off; Freddie gave quite a few interviews talking about Japan. They started thinking about their next album, and we saw quite a lot of them in Trident – there was a lot to talk about. Everything that we at Trident had done for them had been excellent on a creative level, but the costs had been enormous, and the time had come when everyone was querying the costs and the tax situation and so on. We had obviously been aware that there had been some pretty hefty bills. What we had done had been absolutely right, but it had had been *at a cost*.

'But they wanted more money; they felt that the time had come when they should be able to start thinking about buying their own houses. They were "stars" now; that was their frame of mind. They had achieved what they had set out to do, though until then the plan had been that any money that came in should be reinvested in the band. From the very beginning we had all known that Queen would be very successful because their music was so good, but our idea was to keep on reinvesting money in the band whereas they felt that by now they should be getting more money for themselves.'

Having discussed with Dave Thomas and also with Norman Sheffield the group's progress both as a recording band and as a stage act largely in the sequence in which Queen's success developed. I lastly asked Thomas what he thought were their personal strengths; what was it that made them knit so well together both musically and in their private relationships. Earlier in our conversation, he had said that there were frequently moments of tension when tempers snapped, both when preparing for concerts and also while working in the studios.

'I think in the situation that groups have to work in this is unavoidable,' he said. 'Everything has to be planned in such detail when groups go on tour nowadays. All the time you're planning the next show just as you're finishing the last one. There's so much equipment that has to be moved around; so many people who all have to sleep and be fed . . . and the technical problems of siting mixers and spotlights precisely, and having the right height for your lighting trusses, each with about twenty lights. There's always so much that can go wrong . . . even getting equipment off a forty-ton truck and carrying it into a hall without either anyone getting injured or any of the equipment being damaged is a major problem in itself; you'd be surprised how often you find doors that aren't big enough! And all this has to be set up and working before the sound-check begins, and it's a matter of pride with the road crew that it is all working properly before the band themselves arrive . . . if it isn't, tempers may be frayed with the road crew – and the band may be worried when they get to the theatre.'

Whether it was Dave Thomas or Jack Nelson who was travelling on tour with them, he always had the responsibility of seeing that all this was co-ordinated properly.

'There were always dramas,' said Thomas. 'If the road crew hadn't been able to de-rig fast enough the previous night and get out of the hall on time, there'd be an upset, and that might mean them not getting to the next hall on time, which would cause more trouble. Always they'd be such little, niggly things, sometimes arising just because the road crew were tired after not being able to get enough sleep, small problems that would only be a matter of commonsense to the rational mind, but which could rapidly become huge mountains if there was any tension.

'I think one of Queen's problems was that they had very few interests outside music; all their thoughts and energies were concentrated on their work. If they had time to kill travelling between gigs, they might read the trade magazines or John or Brian would get their polaroid cameras out and start taking photographs, but there'd be very little else for them to do or think about other than the next gig . . .

'One of the worst moments we had was just before the Manchester concert when the stage was all set up and all the wiring had been done, and it was only then that Brian – who uses feed-back from his guitar as an effect – found that something was completely throwing his feed-back. We discovered that underneath the stage there was some form of electric cable to a generator system and it was this that was completely throwing the feed-back, so all the earthing of the equipment had to be changed which delayed the sound-check until the first people were actually being let into the theatre. But this is the sort of thing that is bound to happen with such complex equipment.'

I then asked Dave Thomas, just as I had earlier asked Norman Sheffield, to give me his personal impressions of the members of the group.

Of Freddie Mercury, he said: 'He is very single-minded, and very generous; he was always quick to give people presents and to say thank-you when someone had done something for him. He is very sensitive, if not too sensitive, and he always had to be amused. He always had to have something to do and hated being left on his own. He always had to be with people ... after a show he was always the one who would be wanting to go out to dinner, surrounded by lots of people, talking and enjoying himself. He is very dedicated as a musician and as an artist and extremely precise about everything, about his clothes on stage or the lights or the sound system. Everything had to be just right, and I think he loved the show business aspect of it all, the glitter and the tinsel.'

Of Brian May, he said: 'He was very quiet and introverted. He always used to think and worry; a born worrier . . . the whole group are the type of people who worry about everything. They'd be worried whether their baggage had arrived at the hotel or whether the room service had been properly done. If they ordered a cup of tea, they'd be worried in case it wouldn't come . . . and Brian was more like this than any of them, especially about things like guitar strings and whether they were going to be all right. When he found himself being set up as an idol-type of guitar player, the adulation started to worry him. He was concerned whether the audiences would understand what he was trying to do . . . and he'd always be wanting to talk to the people who came along to their concerts in a very genuine way to see what they thought about the band. One funny little thing was that he always had a scarf that he used to prize which had been given to him as a present, and we all had to be on the lookout to make sure that he didn't leave this behind in his dressing room or at a restaurant because we knew how upset he would be if he lost it. On a couple of occasions he had mislaid it, and that had thrown him completely ... it's just another aspect of him being a worrier.'

Of Roger Taylor, he said: 'He loves the showbiz side of it all, too. He had always wanted to be a rock 'n' roll drummer star, and when it all happened to him he was delighted; his dreams had come true. Roger was always the easiest member of the group to please. He was always happy providing the band was playing well and so was he. He was also one of the great comedians who in moments of tension would provide a little light relief. He was a great mimic, and he'd use this to good effect if the tension got a bit hairy. But he never told jokes; none of them are the sort of people who could tell a joke. I think this ability he has to treat things lightly when they could easily get out of hand helped to knit the group together. The thing I used to notice about them was that all four members of the group were always so very loyal to each other. They were very closely knit. They could have the most alarming rows, but the loyalty to one another was always there – and I think that's one of the reasons why they have been so successful. Whenever I look at a new group, that's one of the first things I look for, loyalty, because you know that if success comes the strain will be tremendous and all the work you do could come to nothing if one of them walks out. I don't think that will happen with Queen. In personal terms there are no weak links, and for that reason I think they'll stick together for a long time to come.'

And then finally of John Deacon, Thomas said: 'He is very independent within the group. He was always the first one out of bed in the morning, whereas you might have to call the others at ten am, and then at ten fifteen am, then ten thirty am or later before they'd get up (especially Brian May who hates getting up in the morning) but if you gave John a time for departure next morning, he'd be there in the hotel lobby ready and waiting five or ten minutes early. He is very quiet and very strong, and always very sane. He's a smoothing influence over the other members of the band. If there were rows during a sound-check, it would be John who would approach the matter analytically . . . and outside music, he had a great passion for Queen's Park Rangers, which used to give him something different to think about. He didn't have the total obsession with music, though you still knew that his heart was totally in it. Of them all, I think John's the one that I can see getting a cottage in the country and living a very quiet, peaceful life when the time comes for him to do it.'

CHAPTER SIX

In the next phase of Queen's career, after they had decided to leave Trident, David Croker again became a crucial figure. It was he who was asked by an intermediary to enquire whether John Reid, who was already managing Elton John, would be interested in representing Queen as well. In another exclusive interview, Croker told me how all this came about.

At almost every stage in Queen's development, Croker had had a front row seat – and he stresses himself that this was and is still primarily his relationship with the group, making it clear that he claims no credit for what Queen achieved after EMI had agreed with Trident that they would distribute the group's records.

When that agreement was reached, Croker was then manager of the newly-formed EMI Records label, and in that capacity had been one of the first people to hear the tapes that eventually became Queen's first album.

'I first heard those tapes in the summer of 1972 when Trident brought them to EMI,' he said. 'At that point Queen were among a number of acts that Trident were trying to have released by EMI, and the actual EMI label itself hadn't even been formed. I was involved in A & R for EMI, and when those tapes came in I was dealing mainly with America. Someone thought it would be a really good deal for us to take the three albums that Trident were offering, which to begin with were by Queen, Eugene Wallace, and a group called Skin Alley. The only trouble with the deal was that it was too expensive, and also I'm afraid to say that EMI were not too keen on Skin Alley, though they eventually ended up on the Transatlantic label. I heard Queen and Eugene Wallace but I'm afraid no one liked Skin Alley. That was a stumbling block because what was being proposed was a three-album deal, one from each of the three acts.'

In fact, at that point EMI turned the group down – and so did several other top British record companies.

In the following January Roy Featherstone, one of EMI's top executives, went off to the Midem festival in the South of France which is the annual music business trade fair when managers, record business executives, publishers and other hustlers all try to do big deals for different rights to songs and records. When Featherstone returned to London, he told Croker: 'You know how it is at Midem, after a couple of days you have heard so much that when something comes along that's OK you jump up and down with excitement. Well, I heard a group that did that to me – Queen.'

'I've heard them already,' said Croker, remembering the tapes that had been brought in the previous summer.

'Well, I heard they were about to do a deal with somebody else – so I sent them a telegram saying don't sign anything until I get back from Midem,' said Featherstone.

Following that, he and Croker went to see Jack Nelson, who was then head of the Trident companies, Trident Audio Productions, and who later became Queen's co-manager.

'He gave us this build-up on Queen and Eugene Wallace,' said Croker. 'We also met them all, which was only to be expected – and we agreed on a figure for the deal with Trident which was substantially lower than the one at which they were originally offered to us by Trident after Skin Alley had gone to Transatlantic.

'We had agreed to sign the deal and it was arranged that we should see them performing live at the Marquee. When they came on stage and started to play, they were fantastic – and then after the second number it all plummeted down hill. It was most extraordinary. As they came on, the effect was terrific and as they started the first number I thought, "My God, I am witnessing something brilliant," but then it all started to go wrong. It was one of those dates which never quite gelled, though at the end they retrieved something with "Big Spender" and their rock 'n' roll medley. Overall, though, it was not a good gig, and some of the people from EMI who had gone along to see them were none too keen after that . . . but Roy Feather-stone hadn't been along to the Marquee that night and when we told him that they hadn't been all that good,' he said: "I don't agree with what you tell me. I am going to do the deal." '

It was lucky for Queen that Featherstone felt like that; had he decided otherwise, events may not have moved so favour-ably.

By now Croker had met Mercury, May, Taylor and Deacon several times, and he says: 'I'd always had this feeling that I'd seen Freddie around somewhere without being able to explain it. It was just a feeling I had, that I'd seen him somewhere before. It just so happened that one of the lads who worked in the EMI office had been to school with Brian May, and he used to tell us all, "he's brilliant", but the contact that we'd had with the group hadn't been that close. Eventually, the whole thing was signed and they came in to see me again, and to my surprise Freddie presented me with the artwork that they'd done for the first album. They had done it all themselves, and said quite bluntly: "This is how our album is going to be." They had even designed their own crest, and they told me where they thought it should go on the album sleeve . . . but when the proofs came back from the printers, they were awful. The foot had been cut off the "Queen" emblem, and then it came back with the emblem miles off centre. We had to re-jig the design three times, but eventually it came out just as the group wanted it, with one photograph of Freddie on stage on the front of the sleeve, and then a sort of collage of polaroid photographs on the back. They came into the office with that collage all laid out themselves with the pictures all stuck to a large sheet of board like a noticeboard and said, "That's how we want it to look!" '

'When the first album was released in July 1973, there was an incredibly low initial sale, perhaps because July is not a good time of year for selling records, or maybe because Queen were a new, untried band that no one had heard of in the stores. Anyway, the response from the shops was not good, and it was then that Jack Nelson came in to see Gerry Cord, who was then managing director of EMI. Jack banged his fist on the table, and it got results. That was one of the true moments of being a records-man.

'The sales were so low that he pushed Gerry Cord into taking over the situation himself instead of issuing an instruction down through a chain of command, which was what usually happened. Gerry went out into the general office and got hold of four secretaries and then dictated a telegram which was sent immediately to all EMI's salesmen on the road, some sixty or seventy people, and they all got this telegram telling them to put everything they'd got into getting orders for the Queen album, signed personally by Cord . . . and it got results. The salesmen got the record into the shops, and we suddenly sold four times as many records as we'd sold before, although the sales were still quite low, compared with the sort of sales their albums got later, the whole thing was beginning to work out. After about a week of those telegrams being sent out, we knew that Queen were going to break. A certain buzz hit the building. Their single "Keep Yourself Alive" was getting quite a lot of radio plays, although we just couldn't get it on the play-lists – and then suddenly Radio Luxembourg really went to town on the Queen album.

'About that time, they went out and did a few gigs, and the feed-back was quite incredible. One of these warm-up gigs was at Imperial College at the back of the Albert Hall; the same college that Brian and Roger had rehearsed at regularly as Smile . . . I went down to see them that night, and they were absolutely stunning. I had no doubt after that that they were going to make it. Everything about them was so impressive, the music, their clothes, their assurance on stage. I think it was their presence that impressed me more than anything else – especially Freddie's. I already knew that he was the singer and wrote a lot of their material, but seeing him that night was something quite different . . . he moved a lot, and came across as a very upfront kind of person.

'And then, of course, when they went out and did that tour with Mott the Hoople the same sort of feed-back was coming to us from all over the country; by the time they finished that tour, there was no doubt that they had established themselves as one of the top Second Division bands in the country . . . by then the album was getting very good returns, and as they started recording the *Queen II* album everyone just knew that Queen were going to happen.

'That first album had sold so well that we couldn't understand how it hadn't got into the charts, and then when the second LP was released we had one of those incredible pieces of luck . . . as part of the plan for them to move out of the second division, a solo tour had been set up for early in 1974. The *Queen II* LP was being released to coincide with it, and it had been decided to issue "Seven Seas of Rhye" as a single – and then we were all hit by the three-day week.

'Because of the Government restrictions on electricity, we had only the three days in which to press and package the albums at the factory – and it had been decided that we would make all the records as standard as possible so that we could get as many out each day as we could. Making that decision was a huge piece of internal politics at EMI, and as part of that plan the *Queen II* album was to be released without an inner bag. Jack Nelson came back and told us: "Unless we get an inner bag you won't get the tapes!" And then there was a very tiny mistake in the printing on the sleeve, and the group themselves absolutely insisted that it would have to be put right . . . which just gives you an indication of their attention to detail . . . and it was while all this was going on and Queen themselves were being totally perfectionist (which, incidentally, I think was absolutely right, because I, too, like to buy albums that are a complete and perfect package) that we had this unexpected piece of luck.

'We were trying to get the LP out on time and we had decided on "Seven Seas of Rhye" as the single, and Ronnie Fowler, who was promotion manager at EMI and probably one of Queen's number one fans, always trying to generate enthusiasm for the group within EMI and shouting their praises, took "Seven Seas of Rhye" down to the "Top Of The Pops" production office, and he arrived just at the moment that they'd discovered that a special piece of David Bowie film wouldn't be arriving in time for that week's show. Ronnie persuaded them to listen to the Queen single, and the group were there and then offered a spot on the show in place of the Bowie segment.

'That was on the Tuesday. On the Tuesday night, the group went into Ramport studios and cut the backing tracks to be used on TV, and then on the Wednesday they filmed their spot for "Top Of The Pops", which was shown on the Thursday night – and by the Saturday we'd got the record into the shops. In effect, we'd turned the round in just three days, but we had to do that once we'd got the chance of a "Top Of The Pops". You can't turn down a chance like that.

'The whole effort was pretty exceptional; I don't think EMI had ever rushed out a record at that speed before . . . there was no time to clear all the paperwork. That had to be done later. Everyone said "Do it" – and it was done. After that the LP came out more or less normally without any more troubles.'

It was that single that gave Queen their first hit, and with such an impetus the *Queen II* album sold exceptionally well for some six months after the release of 'Seven Seas of Rhye'.

'In the States another track was released as a single, "Liar", which had been the most requested of all their numbers on the Mott the Hoople tour,' said Croker. 'I think it was very unfortunate for the group that Brian fell ill on that first US tour they did – they could quite easily have broken through there in 1974 if it hadn't been for that.'

Soon afterwards, Croker himself became managing director of Rocket Records, the company that Elton John formed with his manager John Reid, though Rocket operates quite independently of Reid's own company, John Reid Enterprises Ltd. Apart from occasionally meeting each other socially, he had little to do with Queen until late summer 1975.

'When it became known that they were bitching with Trident, I suggested to Freddie that he might like to meet John Reid. I told him, I was sure he would give them a fair deal, but I didn't push the matter; it was really up to them to take any initiative . . . the rumour was going around the business, anyway, that they were looking for a new manager.

'Then one day I was sitting here in my office, at this desk, when the phone rang and someone, I'd rather not say who it was, asked me whether John would be prepared to consider managing Queen. I went downstairs to John's office and told him: "I think there's a chance that Queen would be interested. Would you like to see them?" We discussed the matter for five or ten minutes, and he asked me what I thought of them as a group, and I said how good I thought they were. Then later I phoned this other person back, and Queen came along to our offices to meet John. I'd found myself acting as broker in this situation by accident – and I'm not even sure that "broker" is the right word. I think that any doubts John may have had about the situation I overcame by saying he should do it. I just happen to think they are a brilliant band, and it's the first time I've ever given a recommendation like that about anyone to John Reid – although it just so happens that John met Elton through me. I was a friend of Elton's in the days when he was just songwriting, and he used to come along to EMI where I was working, scrounging records, and John Reid worked with me at the same offices. In fact, originally when we both went to EMI for the first time in July 1969, we had both gone after the same job, and then John later became the Motown label manager while I looked after Bell, and John and I have been friends ever since; so on the days when Elton came into the office, I introduced him to John and that was how it all started.

'I'd always had this feeling about Queen; there's a sort of chemical relationship there just as there was with The Beatles and The Who. You always have that in every band that is going to be huge, there's a good-looking one, a quiet one, a musician and an outrageous one. They're all individuals and quite different to each other, and yet they knit together in the way that all the best groups do . . . and they're also highly intelligent, excellent musicians, and in Freddie and Brian there are two quite outstanding songwriters . . . it's very exciting to see that all coming together in one group.

'The other thing that they have is great strength. They know exactly what they are going to do and what they will not do. They can be very demanding, as artists often can, and are certainly prepared to dig their toes in rather than do something that goes against their grain. They will say quite bluntly, "You are not going to manipulate us."

'And once they've adopted a position like that, you will only get round them by persuading them with reason. When they did that film to promote "Bohemian Rhapsody", there was a lot of politics like that going on in the office. And then eventually Bruce Gowers was brought in to direct with a budget of some £3,200, and I wasn't involved in that at all because I was in Australia at the time, although I do know that the live sequence was filmed at Elstree while they were rehearsing for their tour. I just saw it for the first time when I came back from Australia, and when the film came on I just fell over backwards because it was so brilliantly conceived, and because it carried through ideas they had had two years earlier for the sleeve of their *Queen II* album. But that's their strength; if they have a good idea, they do know how to carry it through, and they're such perfectionists that they'll insist that it's done just as they want it to be done. That's what makes their music stand up.'

CHAPTER SEVEN

When Queen flew back from Tokyo after their first and somewhat surprising tour of Japan, they arrived back in London faced with a clear schedule, although there had been talk between them and Trident of repeating the work-pattern that had been established the previous year, and which had worked so well.

Roughly speaking, the intention was that they should spend the summer months writing, rehearsing and then recording their fourth album and that this should then be released in the autumn of 1975 together with a single and yet another major tour of Britain.

It was a simple time-table, but it had proved itself in late 1974 when they had released the *Sheer Heart Attack* LP and the 'Killer Queen' single, promoting them both with that elaborately staged act which had then been taken around Europe, across the United States, and then on to Japan.

Only one major problem presented itself – the fact that individually Queen thought the time had come when they really should be enjoying the fruits of their success, and the equally apparent truth that it was early days yet. In the sixties, it had taken The Who and The Rolling Stones as long as five years before they had found themselves in the money and able to buy large country houses – but these were the seventies, the finances of rock had changed, and in the public mind Queen were now on a par with groups like that. And in their own minds, too.

The rights and wrongs of the dispute that arose between them and Trident are really no concern of mine, and, anyway, it is still too soon after the event to judge the matter; Norman Sheffield may well be right when he says that he and his colleagues at Trident handled the situation carefully, realising that if they didn't Queen were a high-tension group and that there was a possibility that the group might even split up. Certainly, it had been reported in the press that Brian May had been invited to join Ron and Russell Mael in the part-American group Sparks.

Friends who had known Mercury in his Kensington Market days found that now he was quieter and more self-controlled, and in two separate interviews that he gave at that time soon after arriving back in London it became plain from his answers to journalists' questions that he was toughening up as so many other top rock stars had done in years gone by.

To the London *Evening News* he said: 'The higher up the ladder you go the more vicious you have to be if you want to stop yourself falling off . . . it isn't that I want to be tough and vicious. It is something that is forced upon you. Once you start making big money everyone wants a piece of the action. All the leeches move in and they will suck you dry if you give them half the chance. You have to watch everyone who works for you. If they seem to be taking you for a ride you have to weed them out fast. You can't afford to let anyone get away with anything . . . really any group who wants to survive has to be made up of fairly shrewd businessmen.' And in a somewhat more guarded interview with *Melody Maker*, he said: 'We're in the process of seeing how much money we've got. I've been living in this flat for three years and I'd like to buy a house.'

The simple reality was that after touring the world with great success (but at enormous cost), having had to cut short both their American tours through illness, and having had that one major hit album on which the royalties would not normally arrive for a long time yet, Queen had very little more money in their pockets than they had had in the days when Roger and Freddie were selling second-hand clothes on their stall in Kensington Market.

Mercury was still living in that rented flat in Holland Park with his girlfriend Mary Austin and their cat Thomas, though now surrounded by souvenirs and a growing collection of bric-a-brac; Taylor was still in that same rented apartment in Kew where he had lived since soon after finishing his course at the

North London Polytechnic; May was still ensconced in his flat in Kensington, and Deacon and his wife were still in the house in Fulham that Deacon had moved into long before his marriage. Apart from the way audiences now reacted to their music, nothing much had changed . . . but soon did.

On switching to John Reid's management, the group temporarily moved into a large house in Surrey complete with swimming pool, games room and large barn attached where they could set up their instruments and work until late into the night working on new material for their fourth album. Then in August 1975 they moved en masse down to the Rockfield studios in Monmouthshire to rehearse all their new songs thoroughly before going into the studios to complete what was to be their most expensive project yet, *A Night At The Opera*.

They were now doing what they had done the previous year: planning an autumn blitz.

First, there was the formal announcement that they had left Trident and joined Elton John, Kevin Ayers and Kiki Dee under the management of John Reid; then there was the presentation of gold albums for *Queen II*, silver and gold albums for *Sheer Heart Attack* and silver albums for *Queen* and silver singles for 'Killer Queen' – just reminding everyone that they really had joined the Big League in the past year.

Then, with as much careful planning as the previous autumn, they released the single 'Bohemian Rhapsody' on October 31st; issued the LP *A Night At The Opera* on November 14th, and then began their fourth tour of Britain the following day. Again it had a lavishly constructed stage show complete with firework and lightning-effects and possibly the widest range of lighting theatrics so far presented in a rock show, which they intended to take across the United States and then on to Japan and Australia in the early months of 1976.

And if it all sounds cold and calculated in its execution, well it has to be – this is big business.

Now, their stage act lasts nearly two hours. It costs more to present than ever – just as each album costs more than the last. Instead of starting with 'Now I'm Here', the theatre darkens for an introduction to 'Bohemian Rhapsody', with Mercury's silhouette projected on a large screen – and then the set bursts into life as they reach the rock 'n' roll section of that number, with flashing lights and magnesium flares emphasising the nightmares of the singer who has killed a man and must survive. It is fine music and the songs that follow are by now mostly familiar to their audience; songs like 'Killer Queen', 'The Prophet Song', 'Doing Alright', 'Stone Cold Crazy' and 'Lap Of The Gods', all presented with precision. And they are the justification for all this extravagance, this cunning artifice. It is their music that matters; those sardonic Mercury lyrics and that extraordinary range of guitar sounds that May manages to produce as effectively on stage as he does in the studio. This is the direction that rock music is taking.

And then when one compares their power and vision, humour and emotion, skill and artistry with what the top groups were doing ten years ago when Queen started, it makes one pause to realise that up and down the country now there is another generation of young musicians coming on behind, possibly even trying to make their own guitars and other instruments, as inspired in their way as Brian May, Freddie Mercury, John Deacon and Roger Taylor all were when they first heard Jimi Hendrix.

APPENDIX ONE

THE QUEEN CHRONOLOGY

In compiling this chronology I have had considerable assistance from Tony Brainsby, who kept records of Queen's progress step-by-step, and from the press office at Rocket Records, who have been handling Queen's press and publicity since they moved from Trident to John Reid's management. Wherever possible I have cross-checked the dates given.

1946
September 5 — Freddie Mercury – Frederick Bulsara – born in Zanzibar, son of civil servant Bomi Bulsara and his wife Jer.

1947
July 19 — Brian Harold May born at Gloucester House nursing home, Hampton Hill, Twickenham, son of Harold May and his wife Ruth (*née* Fletcher) of Feltham.

1949
July 26 — Roger Meddows Taylor born at West Norfolk and King's Lynn Hospital, son of Michael Meddows Taylor and his wife Winifred (*née* Hickman).

1951
August 19 — John Richard Deacon born at St Francis's private hospital, London Road, Leicester, son of Arthur Henry Deacon and his wife Lilian Mollie (*née* Perkins).

1952
Brian May starts at the Hanworth Road Primary School, Feltham.

1956

John Deacon starts school at the Oadby infants' school, Leicester, going on to Gartree High School.

1957

Roger Meddows Taylor moves to Truro, Cornwall, with parents and sister Clare and starts at the Cathedral School.

1958
September

Brian May wins a scholarship and starts at Hampton Grammar School.

1959

Freddie Mercury and his parents and his sister Kashmira move to England and settle in a house in Feltham, approximately 100 yards away from Brian May's home.

1960

Roger Meddows Taylor moves on to Truro School, staying there until he is eighteen and playing in local groups.

1962
September

John Deacon starts at Beauchamp Grammar School, Leicester, staying until he is eighteen and playing in local groups.

1963/4

Brian May makes his own guitar with his father's help, and then goes on to form the group 1984 at Hampton Grammar School with Tim Staffell, Dave Dilloway, John Garnham and Richard Thompson.

1966/8

Freddie Mercury and Tim Staffell leave their respective schools and begin courses at

Ealing College of Art; meanwhile, Brian May has gone to Imperial College intending to become an infra-red astronomer. May puts an advertisement on the college board for a drummer – and Roger Meddows Taylor replies. Taylor, May and Staffell form the group Smile.

1969

Smile have their one and only record 'Earth' (written by Staffell) c/w 'Step On Me' (by May and Staffell) released in the US by Mercury Records. John Anthony produces it.

1970

Freddie Mercury joins his first group Wreckage, which occasionally appears under the name Sour Milk Sea – sometimes with Richard Thompson as its drummer.

Summer

Staffell leaves Smile to join Colin Petersen's new group Humpy Bomp. Soon afterwards May and Taylor form the new group Queen with Freddie Mercury as their singer. Meanwhile, Taylor and Mercury have been running their own stall in Kensington Market.

1971
February

John Deacon joins Queen; the last person to join the group, who make their first recordings at De Lane Lea studios where they are asked by a friend to test some new equipment. Among the tracks they record are 'Liar'. These tapes are later played by John Anthony to executives at Trident Audio Productions.

1972
November 1   Queen sign record production, management and publishing contracts with Trident and Jack Nelson becomes their manager; later Dave Thomas becomes co-manager.

1973
March   EMI forms its own record label, EMI, its first releases being by The Real Thing, Johnny Johnson, Geordie and Hurricane Smith.

April 6   David Croker, then EMI label manager, issues internal memo: '*RE QUEEN*: We have just entered into agreement whereby we will be releasing records by the above group. Trident Studios have arranged a special performance by the band on Monday 9th April at the Marquee Club. I would be grateful if as many people as possible could see their way clear to attend . . .'

June   Release of Freddie Mercury's first single – under the name Larry Lurex. Single is titled 'I Can Hear Music' (by Greenwich, Spector and Barry) c/w 'Goin' Back' (by Goffin and King). This was a Trident Audio production, produced by Robin Geoffrey Cable.

July 6   Release of Queen's first single 'Keep Yourself Alive' (written by Brian May) c/w 'Son and Daughter' (May) (EMI). Both tracks were taken from their first LP.

July 13   Release of the group's first album *Queen*. Tracks: 'Liar' (Mercury), 'The Night Comes Down' (May), 'Modern Times Rock 'N' Roll' (Taylor), 'Son and Daughter' (May), 'Jesus' (Mercury), 'Seven Seas of Rhye' (Mercury), 'Keep Yourself Alive' (May), 'Doing All Right' (May and Staffell), 'Great King Rat' (Mercury) and 'My Fairy King' (Mercury). The album was

	produced by John Anthony and Roy Thomas Baker.
August 15	Group begin work on their second album at Trident Studios.
September 13	Appear on live 'In Concert' show at Golders Green Hippodrome.
	Appear at the Imperial College, Kensington, where Brian May and Roger Taylor had often been booked in the past when in Smile.
September 24	Bob Harris features them on his 'Sounds of the 70's' BBC stereo radio programme; the first of many Queen spots on the show.
October 1	Film a promotional film for one of the Trident companies.
October 11–13	Queen make TV appearances in Belgium, France and Holland.
October 14	'In Concert' programme on Radio Luxembourg.
October 20	On BBC Radio One programme also called 'In Concert'
November 12	Queen begin their first major tour at Leeds Town Hall as supporting act to Mott the Hoople.
November 13	Blackburn St George's.
November 15	Worcester Gaumont.
November 16	Lancaster University.
November 17	Liverpool Stadium.
November 18	Stoke-on-Trent Trentham Gardens.
November 19	Wolverhampton Civic.
November 20	Oxford New Theatre.
November 21	Preston Guildhall.
November 22	Newcastle City Hall.
November 23	Glasgow Apollo Centre.
November 25	Edinburgh Caley Cinema.
November 26	Manchester Opera House.
November 27	Birmingham Town Hall.
November 28	Swansea Brangwyn Hall.
November 29	Bristol Colston.
November 30	Bournemouth Winter Gardens.

December 1	Southend Kursaal.
December 2	Chatham Central.
December 14	Hammersmith Odeon (final date of their tour with Mott the Hoople).

1974

January 5	In the annual *Sounds* music paper poll Queen are voted third in Best New Artist section (British) and ninth Best New (International.)
January/February	Queen fly to Australia and appear twice at a three-day open air music festival in Melbourne. When they return to London, there are twelve photographers waiting – and they walk away without taking any photos on discovering it is not *the* Queen.
February	Voted second most promising act of the year in annual *New Musical Express* poll; Leo Sayer was first.
February 23	John Deacon tells *Record Mirror*: 'We're a hard, heavy electric rock band with quite a bit of melody and complex harmonies . . . a lot of people have been comparing us with Led Zeppelin, but whereas they're into straight ahead rock, we're more structured and a lot more intricate planning goes into our music especially in the recording studios.'
February 25	Release of second single 'Seven Seas of Rhye' (Mercury), which was a different version to that heard on the first LP. The B-side was 'See What A Fool I've Been' (EMI).
March 1	Queen begin their first bill-topping tour at Blackpool Winter Gardens supported by Nutz.
March 2	Aylesbury Friars.
March 3	Plymouth Guildhall – when they are late going on stage the audience begin singing 'God Save The Queen', which soon becomes a feature of their concerts.

March 4	Paignton Festival Hall
March 8	Release of their second LP *Queen II* by EMI. Tracks: 'Ogre Battle', 'The Fairy Feller's Master-Stroke', 'Nevermore', 'The March of the Black Queen', 'Funny How Love Is' and 'Seven Seas of Rhye' (Mercury), and 'Procession' (May), 'Father To Son' (May), 'White Queen (As It Began)' (May), 'Some Day One Day' (May) and 'The Loser In The End' (Taylor). All tracks were produced by Roy Thomas Baker and Queen except 'Nevermore' and 'Funny How Love Is' (produced by Robin Geoffrey Cable and Queen) and 'The March of the Black Queen' (produced by Roy Thomas Baker, Robin Geoffrey Cable and Queen).
March 8	Sunderland Locarno.
March 9	Cambridge Corn Exchange.
March 10	Croydon Greyhound.
March 12	Dagenham Roundhouse.
March 14	Cheltenham Town Hall.
March 15	Glasgow University.
March 16	Stirling University – rioting starts after the group have done three encores and the crowd still want more. Two people are stabbed. Two members of the Queen road crew end up in hospital. Queen have to cancel a concert the following night at Birmingham Barbarella's.
March 19	Cleethorpes Winter Gardens.
March 20	Manchester University.
March 23	Cromer Links Pavilion.
March 24	Colchester Woods Leisure Centre.
March 26	Douglas Palace Lido, Isle of Man.
March 28	Aberystwyth University.
March 29	Penzance Winter Gardens.
March 30	Taunton Century Ballroom.
March 31	London Rainbow.
April 2	Birmingham Barbarella's (replacing concert originally set for March 17).

April 12	Leave for six-week US tour, opening in Denver, Colorado, as support act to Mott the Hoople.
May	Group appear for a week with Mott the Hoople at the Uris Theatre, Broadway, New York – the first rock group to star on Broadway. They are due to go on to Boston after the final show, but Brian May collapses with hepatitis.
May 16	Brian May flown back to London and doctors order him to hospital.
June 15	After May's illness, Mercury tells *New Musical Express*: 'We thought he had food poisoning. Then he went yellow. The doctor freaked and we all had jabs.' All the journalists, musicians and record company staff who had come into contact with May were also inoculated.
July 15	After a week's rehearsals at Rockfield Studios, Monmouthshire, Queen begin recording their third LP at Trident.
August 2	Brian May taken ill and rushed to hospital again – and has operation for duodenal ulcer. The band have to cancel a US tour planned for September. Meanwhile, Queen continue recording without May, leaving his parts to be added later.
August 11	Members of the group attend EMI Records–Radio Luxembourg motor racing rally at Brands Hatch.
September 5	Group presented with Silver Disc for sales of *Queen II* – by 'Queen' Jeanette Charles, the model who looks like Queen Elizabeth. The reception was at the Café Royal and was their first appearance in public since May's illness in the US.
October 11	Release of their third single 'Killer Queen' (Mercury), a double-A side coupled with 'Flick Of The Wrist' (Mercury). Both tracks were taken from their forthcoming LP *Sheer Heart Attack* (EMI).

October 18	Queen presented with engraved tankards by their publishers, Feldmans, to mark their success in Britain and the US.
October 30	Queen begin a British tour at Manchester Palace supported by Hustler.
October 31	Hanley Victoria Hall.
November 1	Liverpool Empire.
November 1	Release of their third LP *Sheer Heart Attack* (EMI). Tracks: 'Brighton Rock' (May), 'Killer Queen' (Mercury), 'Tenement Funster' (Taylor), 'Flick Of The Wrist' (Mercury), 'Lily Of The Valley' (Mercury), 'Now I'm Here' (May), 'In The Lap Of The Gods' (Mercury), 'Stone Cold Crazy' (May, Mercury, Taylor, Deacon), 'Dear Friends' (May), 'Misfire' (Deacon), 'Bring Back That Leroy Brown' (Mercury), 'She Makes Me (Stormtrooper In Stilettoes)' (May) and 'In The Lap Of The Gods . . . Revisited' (Mercury). Produced by Roy Thomas Baker and Queen.
November 2	Leeds University.
November 2	Talking of 'Killer Queen', Mercury tells the *New Musical Express*: 'It's about a high class call girl. I'm trying to say that classy people can be whores as well.'
November 3	Coventry Theatre.
November 4	Coventry Theatre.
November 5	Sheffield City Hall.
November 6	Bradford St George's Hall.
November 7	Newcastle City Hall.
November 8	Glasgow Apollo Centre.
November 9	Lancaster University.
November 10	Preston Guildhall.
November 11	Preston Guildhall.
November 12	Bristol Colston.
	'Killer Queen' reaches number one in the *Melody Maker* chart.
November 13	Bournemouth Winter Gardens.
November 14	Southampton Guildhall.
November 15	Swansea Brangwyn Hall.

November 16	Birmingham Town Hall.
November 17	Birmingham Town Hall.
November 18	Oxford New Theatre.
November 19	London Rainbow.
November 20	London Rainbow – concert arranged when all tickets for the first concert sold out in two days. Both concerts were video-taped and later edited into a thirty-three minute film 'Queen At The Rainbow'.
November 22– December 10	Begin European tour with concerts in Sweden, Norway, Finland, Denmark, Germany, Switzerland, France, Belgium and Holland.
December 25	Appear on special Christmas Day edition of '45' (Granada TV).

1975

January 17	Release of fourth British single 'Now I'm Here' (Brian May) and 'Lily Of The Valley' (Mercury) – both tracks taken from the *Sheer Heart Attack* LP (EMI).
January 18	John Deacon marries Veronica Agnes Mary Tetzlaff, a school teacher, at the Carmelite Church in Kensington.
January 25	In the *Record Mirror* poll Queen are voted number two in the British Newcomer section; 'Killer Queen' is voted number two single of the past year in the British section and number nine in the International section.
January 31	The group leaves for the States, having spent much of January editing their Rainbow film.
February 5	US tour begins at Columbus Agora, Ohio.
February 6	Cincinatti Reflections.
February 7	Dayton Palace Theatre, Ohio.
February 8	In the *New Musical Express* poll Queen are voted eighth in the Top British Group section; seventh Best Stage Band; third in Most Promising New Name; seventeenth

	World Group, and fourth Most Promising in World section.
February 8	Cleveland Music Hall, Ohio.
February 9	South Bend Marric Civic Auditorium, Indiana.
February 10	Detroit Ford Auditorium.
February 11	Toledo Student Union Auditorium.
February 12	Day off.
February 13	Day off.
February 14	Waterbury Palace Theatre, Connecticut.
February 15	Boston Orpheum Theatre.
February 16	New York Avery Fisher Hall.
February 17	Trenton War Memorial, New Jersey.
February 18	Day off.
February 19	Lewiston, Maine.
February 21	Passaic, New Jersey.
February 22	Harrisburg, Pennsylvania.
February 23	Philadelphia Erlinger Theatre – after the show Freddie is taken to a throat specialist, barely able to speak.
February 24	Washington John F. Kennedy Center – and then concerts scheduled for Pittsburgh, Kutzton, Buffalo, Toronto, Kitchener, London and Davenport are cancelled so that Freddie can rest his voice.
March 5	Tour resumes at Mary E. Sawyer Auditorium, La Crosse.
March 6	Madison, Wisconsin.
March 7	Milwaukee Uptown Theatre.
March 8	Chicago Aragon Ballroom.
March 9	St Louis Kiel Ballroom.
March 10	Fort Wayne Coliseum.
March 12	Atlanta Municipal Auditorium.
March 13	Charlestown Civic Auditorium.
March 14	Concert at Florida Citrus Showcase, Winter Haven, cancelled to rest Freddie's voice.
March 15	Miami Marina, Florida.
March 18	Concert at St Bernards Auditorium, New Orleans, cancelled to rest Freddie's voice.
March 20	San Antonio Municipal Hall.
March 21	Houston Music Hall.

March 22	Concert at Austin Armadillo World cancelled so that Freddie can rest his voice.
March 23	Dallas McFarlin Auditorium.
March 25	Concert at Tulsa Municipal Theatre cancelled so that Freddie can rest his voice.
March 26	Concert at Kansas Municipal Auditorium cancelled so that Freddie can rest his voice.
March 29	Santa Monica Civic Auditorium.
March 30	San Francisco Winterland.
April 2	Edmonton.
April 3	Calgary.
April 5	Concert in Vancouver cancelled so that Freddie can rest his voice.
April 6	Seattle.
April 7	Concert in Portland, which was to have been final date of tour, cancelled – and then Queen go to Kavai in the Hawaiian islands for a ten-day holiday. When they arrive in Tokyo they find nearly 3,000 fans waiting at the airport and that 'Killer Queen' is number one in the Japanese music magazine charts.
April 19	Tokyo Budokan.
April 22	Aichi Taiikukan, Nagoya.
April 23	Nokusai Kaikan, Kobe.
April 25	Kyuden Taiikukan, Fukuoka.
April 28	Okayama Taiikukan, Okayama.
April 29	Yamaha Tsumagoi Hall, Shizuoka.
April 30	Bunka Taiikukan, Yokohama.
May 1	Tokyo Budokan.
May 17	In the annual *Disc* poll Queen win four sections – and are voted Top Live Group, Top International Group, Top British Group and 'Killer Queen' is voted Best Single of The Past Year. Their LP *Sheer Heart Attack* is voted number three in the Best Album section.
May 24	In a *Melody Maker* interview, Freddie Mercury says: 'We're in the process of seeing how much money we've got. I've been

	living in this flat for three years and I'd like to buy a house.'
June 18	Freddie Mercury tells the London *Evening News*: 'The higher up the ladder you go the more vicious you have to be if you want to stop yourself falling off.'
August 16	Reported in the music paper *Sounds* that John Reid is now managing Queen 'since they have split with their previous management'. Reid was already managing Elton John.
September 6	Reported in the *New Musical Express*: 'Strong rumours of an imminent split in the ranks of Queen were vehemently denied by their press representative this week. A spokesman said: "There is no question of them breaking up – the band are currently recording an album for November release and hope to tour later in the year.'
September 19	At a London reception to mark their management agreement with John Reid, the group are presented with Silver and Gold discs for sales of the 'Killer Queen' single, Silver and Gold Discs for the *Sheer Heart Attack* LP, a Gold Disc for the *Queen II* LP and a Silver Disc for *Queen* LP.
September 27	In a *New Musical Express* interview, Mercury says of their former management: 'As far as Queen are concerned they are deceased. They cease to exist in any capacity with us whatsoever. One leaves them behind like one leaves excreta. We feel so relieved . . . we felt there came a time when we had got far too big for them to handle.'
October 31	Release of the fifth Queen single 'Bohemian Rhapsody' (Mercury) c/w 'I'm In Love With My Car' (Taylor). This stays at number one in the British music paper charts for eight weeks – something that no other record had done in twenty years. Both

	tracks were taken from the LP *A Night At The Opera* (EMI).
November 7	The LP is previewed with a reception at the Roundhouse Studios, where it is said to have cost £30,000–£40,000 to make. This made it one of the most expensive LPs ever produced in Britain.
November 14	*A Night At The Opera* LP released by EMI. Tracks: 'Death On Two Legs' (Mercury), 'Lazing On A Sunday Afternoon' (Mercury), 'I'm In Love With My Car' (Taylor), 'You're My Best Friend' (Deacon), '39' (May), 'Sweet Lady' (May), 'Seaside Rendezvous' (Mercury), 'The Prophet's Song' (May), 'Love Of My Life' (Mercury), 'Good Company' (May) and 'Bohemian Rhapsody' (Mercury). The LP was produced at Sarm, Roundhouse, Olympic, Rockfield, Scorpio and Lansdowne Studios by Roy Thomas Baker and Queen.
November 14	Queen begin British tour with the first of two concerts at Liverpool Empire. Supported throughout by Mr Big.
November 15	Liverpool Empire.
November 16	Coventry Theatre.
November 17	Bristol Colston.
November 18	Bristol Colston.
November 19	Cardiff Capitol.
November 21	Taunton Odeon.
November 23	Bournemouth Winter Gardens.
November 24	Southampton Gaumont.
November 26	Manchester Free Trade Hall.
November 27	Manchester Free Trade Hall.
November 29	London Hammersmith Odeon.
November 30	London Hammersmith Odeon.
December 1	London Hammersmith Odeon.
December 2	London Hammersmith Odeon.
December 7	Wolverhampton Civic Hall.
December 8	Preston Guildhall.
December 9	Birmingham Odeon.
December 10	Birmingham Odeon.

December 11	Newcastle City Hall.
December 13	Dundee Caird Hall.
December 14	Aberdeen Capitol.
December 15	Glasgow Apollo.
December 16	Glasgow Apollo.
December 24	London Hammersmith Odeon – this special Christmas Eve concert was televised live on 'Old Grey Whistle Test' (BBC-2).

1976

January 14	After 'Bohemian Rhapsody' has been eight weeks at number one in the music paper charts, John Reid announces that it has sold over 1,000,000 copies in Britain alone and that the LP has also sold over 500,000 copies.
January 27	Queen begin their third US tour at the Waterbury Palace Theatre, Connecticut.
January 29	Boston Music Hall.
January 30	Boston Music Hall.
January 31	Philadelphia Tower Theatre.
February 1	Philadelphia Tower Theatre.
February 2	Philadelphia Tower Theatre.
February 5	New York Beacon Theatre.
February 6	New York Beacon Theatre.
February 7	New York Beacon Theatre.
February 8	New York Beacon Theatre.
February 11	Detroit Masonic Temple.
February 13	Cincinatti Riverfront Coliseum.
February 14	Cleveland Public Hall.
February 14	In the annual *New Musical Express* poll Queen are voted number one British Stage Band, number two Group, number five World Group, number three World Stage Band; Mercury is voted number seven World Singer, Brian May third Top Guitarist; 'Bohemian Rhapsody' is voted number one single of the past year and the LP *A Night At The Opera* number two Album.
February 14	In the *Record Mirror and Disc* poll, Queen are voted number one British Group;

'Bohemian Rhapsody', number one single; Freddie Mercury, number six World Singer and number five British Singer; Mercury, number five British Songwriter and number seven World Songwriter; Brian May, number four British Musician and number four World Musician, and *A Night At The Opera* is voted number six in the Best LP section.

February 15	Toledo Sports Arena.
February 18	Saginaw Civic Center, Michigan.
February 19	Columbus Veterans Memorial Auditorium, Ohio.
February 22	Chicago Auditorium.
February 23	Chicago Auditorium.
February 26	Kiel Auditorium, St Louis.
February 27	Indianapolis Convention Center.
February 28	Dane County Coliseum, Madison, Wisconsin.
February 29	Fort Wayne Coliseum, Indiana.
March 1	Milwaukee Auditorium.
March 3	Minneapolis St Paul's Auditorium.
March 7	Berkeley Community Theatre, California.
March 9	Santa Monica Civic Auditorium.
March 10	Santa Monica Civic Auditorium.
March 11	Santa Monica Civic Auditorium.
March 12	Santa Monica Civic Auditorium.
March 20	Arrive in Japan for their second Japanese tour.
March 21	Reception by Japanese record company.
March 22	Tokyo.
March 23	Nagoya.
March 25	Remeji.
March 29	Okara.
March 30	Tokyo.
March 31	Tokyo.
April 2	Sendai.
April 11	Begin Australian tour in Perth.
April 14	Adelaide.
April 17	Sydney.
April 18	Sydney.

April 19	Melbourne.
April 20	Melbourne.
April 22	Brisbane.
April 23	Brisbane – and then the group were due to return to Britain to begin writing and rehearsing material for their fifth LP which was due to be released in autumn 1976.

APPENDIX TWO

Every rock star must have his 'life-lines' – the neat, capsuled summary of biographical details that gives you his personality at-a-glance. These are always, but always, issued to the music papers, teenage magazines, national and provincial press. And Queen were no different. As soon as they started promoting their first singles, Freddie Mercury, Brian May, Roger Taylor and John Deacon each filled in the standard questionnaire in his own hand-writing. I have photo-copies of their original answers. This was how they completed the forms:

NAME: Brian May
DATE OF BIRTH: July 19th, 1947
HEIGHT: 6ft 1 in
WEIGHT: 10½ stones
COLOUR OF HAIR: Dark brown
COLOUR OF EYES: Hazel
FAVOURITE COLOUR: Black
FAVOURITE MUSICIAN: John Lennon, Jimi Hendrix
FAVOURITE GROUP: The Beatles
FAVOURITE ALBUMS: *Abbey Road* (Beatles), *Band of Gypsies* (Jimi Hendrix)
FAVOURITE BOOKS: *Steppenwolf* by Hermann Hesse. *The Glass Bead Game*
FAVOURITE MAGAZINE: *Disneyland*
FAVOURITE WRITER (NOVELIST OR POET): Hermann Hesse, C S Lewis
FAVOURITE MOVIES: 'Women In Love'
FAVOURITE ACTOR: James Mason
FAVOURITE ACTRESS: Natalie Wood
COUNTRY YOU LOVE BEST: England
FAVOURITE FOOD: Vegetarian and prawn cocktails
FAVOURITE DRINK: Grapefruit juice
MUSIC WHICH INFLUENCED YOU MOST: Who-Hendrix-Cream-Beatles
FAVOURITE INSTRUMENT: Guitar

INSTRUMENT YOU PLAY ON STAGE (in detail): Home made guitar, Stratocaster
AMPLIFIER/OTHER DEVICE, EQUIPMENT: AC30s, various delay machines
WHAT WERE YOU DOING BEFORE YOU STARTED PLAYING PROFESSIONALLY: Research in astronomy
YOUR DREAM: Total understanding between people
GROUPS AND TYPE OF MUSIC YOU HATE: Carpenters, Johnny Mathis
SPECIAL TALENT OTHER THAN MUSIC: Inventing

NAME: Freddie Mercury
DATE OF BIRTH: September 5th, 1946
HEIGHT: 5ft 9¾in
WEIGHT: 8½ stones
COLOUR OF HAIR: Midnight black
COLOUR OF EYES: Liquid brown
FAVOURITE COLOUR: Black
FAVOURITE MUSICIAN: Jimi Hendrix
FAVOURITE GROUP: Mott the Hoople
FAVOURITE ALBUMS: *Imagine* (John Lennon)
FAVOURITE BOOKS: *Peter Rabbit* (B Potter)
FAVOURITE MAGAZINES: *Luster Cluster Weekly, Jeremy*
FAVOURITE WRITER (NOVELIST OR POET): B Potter, Richard Dadd
FAVOURITE MOVIES: Any Mae West movie
FAVOURITE ACTOR: —
FAVOURITE ACTRESS: Liza Minelli
COUNTRY YOU LOVE THE BEST: Japan
FAVOURITE FOOD: Nectar
FAVOURITE DRINK: Champagne in a glass slipper
MUSIC WHICH INFLUENCED YOU MOST: Varied
MUSICIANS WHICH INFUENCED YOU MOST: Paganini, Hendrix
FAVOURITE INSTRUMENT: Harpsicord
INSTRUMENT YOU PLAY ON STAGE (IN DETAIL): Piano (Grand)
AMPLIFIER/OTHER DEVICE, EQUIPMENT: Helpenstill pick-up for piano
WHAT WERE YOU DOING BEFORE YOU STARTED PLAYING PROFESSIONALLY: A Kensington poseur

YOUR DREAM: To remain the divine, lush creature that I am
GROUPS AND TYPES OF MUSIC YOU HATE: Tedious rock bands
SPECIAL TALENT OTHER THAN MUSIC: Ponsing and poovery

NAME: John Deacon
DATE OF BIRTH: August 19th, 1951
HEIGHT: 5ft 11in
WEIGHT: 9st 10lbs
COLOUR OF HAIR: Dark brown
COLOUR OF EYES: Green/grey
FAVOURITE COLOUR: Black
FAVOURITE MUSICIAN: None
FAVOURITE GROUP: Gonzalas
FAVOURITE ALBUMS: *Queen II*
FAVOURITE BOOKS: Science fiction
FAVOURITE MAGAZINE: *Men Only*
FAVOURITE WRITER (NOVELIST OR POET): None
FAVOURITE MOVIES: 'Clockwork Orange', 'The Prime of Miss Jean Brodie'
FAVOURITE ACTOR: None
FAVOURITE ACTRESS: None
COUNTRY YOU LOVE BEST: England
FAVOURITE FOOD: Cheese on toast
FAVOURITE DRINK: Milk
MUSIC WHICH INFLUENCED YOU MOST: Rock
MUSICIANS WHICH INFLUENCED YOU MOST: Chris Squires, Philip Chen
FAVOURITE INSTRUMENT: Bass guitar
INSTRUMENT YOU PLAY ON STAGE (IN DETAIL): Bass guitar
AMPLIFIER/OTHER DEVICE, EQUIPMENT: Acoustic 370/Hiwatt 100+2x (4×12) cabs
WHAT WERE YOU DOING BEFORE YOU STARTED PLAYING PROFESSIONALLY: Student (electronics)
YOUR DREAM: Wet
GROUPS AND TYPE OF MUSIC YOU HATE: Country/folk
SPECIAL TALENT OTHER THAN MUSIC: Electronics genius/car mechanic

141

NAME: Roger Taylor
DATE OF BIRTH: July 26th, 1949
HEIGHT: 5ft 10in
WEIGHT: 9½ stones
COLOUR OF HAIR: Blond
COLOUR OF EYES: Blue
FAVOURITE COLOUR: Silver
FAVOURITE MUSICIAN: Jimi Hendrix
FAVOURITE GROUP: The Who
FAVOURITE ALBUMS: *Electric Ladyland*, The Beatles' *White Album*
FAVOURITE BOOKS: *On The Road* (Jack Kerouac), *Dune* (Frank Herbert)
FAVOURITE MAGAZINE: *Queen* (what else?)
FAVOURITE WRITER (NOVELIST OR POET): Jack Kerouac, C S Lewis
FAVOURITE MOVIES: '2001', 'A Clockwork Orange', 'King Kong', 'The Great Race'
FAVOURITE ACTOR: Tony Curtis
FAVOURITE ACTRESS: Jane Fonda
COUNTRY YOU LOVE BEST: Don't know till I've seen them all
FAVOURITE FOOD: Japanese
FAVOURITE DRINK: Southern Comfort
MUSIC WHICH INFLUENCED YOU MOST: Guitar music since 1950. Rock – especially Hendrix and Dylan
MUSICIANS WHICH INFLUENCED YOU MOST: Hendrix, Hank Marvin, John Bonham, David Bowie
FAVOURITE INSTRUMENT: Drums
INSTRUMENT YOU PLAY ON STAGE (IN DETAIL): Drums – large 5 drum Ludwig kit with 26 inch bass drum and assorted percussion
AMPLIFIER/OTHER DEVICE, EQUIPMENT: —
WHAT WERE YOU DOING BEFORE YOU STARTED PLAYING PROFESSIONALLY: Dental then biology student
YOUR DREAMS: To be rich, famous, happy and popular and everything else everyone wants to be but won't admit to
GROUPS AND TYPES OF MUSIC YOU HATE: Osmonds, Carpenters, Ray Conif (sic) and other such muzak rubbish
SPECIAL TALENT OTHER THAN MUSIC: Academic and good talker/Bullshitter